60 SECONDS
for JESUS

Also by Father Jim Sichko

Encountering God:
As a Traveling Papal Missionary of Mercy

Among Friends:
Stories from the Journey

60 SECONDS for JESUS

ONE MINUTE A DAY CAN CHANGE YOUR LIFE

LOYOLA PRESS.
A JESUIT MINISTRY
Chicago

FATHER JIM SICHKO

LOYOLA PRESS.
A JESUIT MINISTRY

www.loyolapress.com

© 2023 Jim Sichko, SJ
All rights reserved.

https://www.biblegateway.com/versions/New-Revised-Standard-Version-Catholic-Edition-NRSVCE-Bible/#booklist

Cover art credit: TopVectors/iStock/Getty Images and Loyola Press

ISBN-13: 978-0-8294-5807-7
Library of Congress Control Number: 2023946931

Printed in the United States of America.
23 24 25 26 27 Versa 10 9 8 7 6 5 4 3 2 1

To my Mom,

who will forever and always be in my heart.

A NOTE FOR YOU

Dear Reader,

What a joy it is to connect with you through these pages! The love of God wraps us in his warmth as we embark on this journey together. Today, I find myself reflecting on the smallest moments of our everyday lives—the times when we've extended a hand of kindness not because we were asked to, but simply because we felt called to do so. Moments filled with simple joys. Laughter and togetherness. Feeling welcome and being welcoming to others. The quiet whispers and reflections between us and God, even if for only a few seconds. As we journey together through this devotional, these are the moments I hope to explore and encourage.

This book isn't about grandiose revelations or theological complexities. Instead, it's about finding the divine in the details, the holy in the humdrum of our daily routines. It's about realizing that every gentle word spoken, every moment of compassion, and every act of love are testaments to the gospel's living power.

We are all beautifully and wonderfully made in God's image. Therefore, whenever we show kindness and extend love, we reflect the very face of God to the world. But more than that, we are the eyes, ears, and hands of God—we are the Body of Christ. That's the heart of our mission, and it's why we're here—to *embody* the love God has for us and to *be* that love in the world. It's my hope that this devotional will serve as a daily reminder of that mission, guiding us toward living the gospel in the most basic, heartfelt ways.

Every day, we're pulled in a thousand different directions. We're inundated with tasks, obligations, pressures, worries, and distractions. But what if, amid that whirlwind, we take just sixty seconds each day to center ourselves in Jesus, to remind ourselves of his mercy, his love, and his call for us to love one another? To live with more joy and meaning? This is the purpose of *60 Seconds for Jesus*. It's an invitation to pause, to breathe, to reflect, and to discover ways we can share God's love in our everyday lives. It's a guide to help you live more intentionally as a disciple of Christ, taking small but significant steps each day to spread joy, love, and kindness.

In the pages that follow, you'll find stories, quotes, musings, and reflections to ponder. You'll also find a few jokes here and there. Why jokes? Well, I think that when we laugh, when we smile, and when we roll our eyes at bad jokes, Jesus is right there with us. So take this book seriously, but remember that not everything in the world is serious.

In the end, it's not the grand gestures but the simple, sincere acts of love that truly matter. As we go through our days, let's remember to spread a little more love and a little more kindness. Just a minute of your day, dear friends, can make a world of difference. This is our call; this is our mission. Together, let us embrace this calling.

As you embark on this journey of *60 Seconds for Jesus,* each week you will be challenged in a new way to come closer to Christ by devoting at least sixty seconds to Jesus each day. Sixty seconds to reflect. To smile, and maybe even laugh. To love. To return to joy.

May you be blessed, and may you in turn be a blessing to others.

Peace and all good,
Father Jim Sichko

CHALLENGE #1

Love is patient; love is kind; love is not envious or boastful or arrogant or rude. It does not insist on its own way; it is not irritable or resentful; it does not rejoice in wrongdoing, but rejoices in the truth. 1 Corinthians 13:4–6

IT'S EASIER THAN EVER TO GET WRAPPED UP IN OUR DAILY lives. So many things are attracting our attention: Our jobs. Expectations. Family. Friends. Social media. Household chores. Watching television. Running errands. You name it! Our lives are filled with distractions that pull our focus away from God. I challenge you to refocus your attention, if only for sixty seconds every day, on the word of God and the life and example of Jesus.

By centering your thoughts on Jesus at least once during the day, Jesus will walk with you, close at hand and near to your heart, throughout the rest of your day. This book is a great way to invite Jesus into your day. You can toss the book into your purse or carry it in a pocket. You can go through it in sequence. Or you can flip to any page on any given day and find a few words and a moment's reflection between you and God.

THIS WEEK'S CHALLENGE:
Decide to devote sixty seconds to Jesus,
every day, for an entire year.

SUNDAY

Take a moment to think about all the challenges you have faced. The ones no one even knows about. And here you are. I hope you are proud of yourself for how far you have come. Be graceful with and gentle on yourself. You're doing amazing.

Monday

Use your voice for kindness,
your ears for compassion,
your hands for charity,
your mind for truth,
and your heart for love.

Tuesday

Stop wishing.
Start doing.
Put work boots on your wish.
Get it done.

Wednesday

Say these words with me,
aloud, and repeat three times:
When I am weak, God is strong.
Where I lack, God will supply.
What I fear, God will love me
through. Today, and every day.
In Jesus' name, I pray.

Thursday

Surround yourself with people
who push you to do and be
better. No drama or negativity.
Just higher goals and higher
motivation. Good times and
positive energy. No jealousy or
hate. Simply bringing out the
absolute best in each other.

Friday

Even though there are days
I wish I could change some
things that happened in the
past, there's a reason the
rearview mirror is so small and
the windshield so big. Where
you are headed is much more
important than what you have
left behind.

Saturday

People ask, "Do I really need Jesus to get into heaven?"
Friend, you need Jesus just to get to the grocery store.

MY 60-SECOND *Reflection*

CHALLENGE #2

While they were talking about this, Jesus himself stood among

them and said to them, "Peace be with you." Luke 24:36

PEACE BE WITH YOU. *AS-SALAAM ALAIKUM. SHALOM ALEICHEM. Om shanti.* Exchanging peace is integral to many religions and evident in global greetings. For Catholics at Mass, sharing a sign of peace is pivotal before receiving communion. Yet, its ubiquity might make the gesture seem mundane.

Peace is both a state of being and a mindset. Feel God's presence and peace, uplifting and supporting you daily.

Let us reflect on the Prayer of St. Francis:
Lord, make me an instrument of your peace:
where there is hatred, let me sow love;
where there is injury, pardon;
where there is doubt, faith;
where there is despair, hope;
where there is darkness, light;
where there is sadness, joy.

THIS WEEK'S CHALLENGE:
May peace be with you, and may you bring peace
to those you encounter.

SUNDAY

In the midst of whatever disappointments, challenges, trials, and sorrows you encounter today, take a step back and take a breath. Say a prayer and remember how much God loves you. Be at peace. In the end, everything will be okay.

Monday

Christian? Yeah.
Perfect? Nah.
Changed? Yeah.
Mistake-free? Nah.
Forgiven? Yeah.
Worthy? Nah.
Accepted? Yeah.
Deserving? Nah.
Loved? Yeah.

Tuesday

The 4 Cs in life: Christ, Choice, Chance, Change. You must make the Choice, to take the Chance, if you want anything in life to Change, and it all becomes possible with Christ.

Wednesday

Got a speeding ticket at sixteen years old. Publicly slipped on a banana peel at nineteen. Still graduated seminary with a 3.92 GPA. God's plan.

Thursday

A baby rabbit gifted a flower to its mother, saying, "I had picked this flower for you, but then I forgot and ate the top."

"That's okay," said the mother rabbit with a laugh. "Love doesn't have to be perfect. It just has to be real."

Friday

In the Gospel of Luke quoted above, Christ challenges the Pharisees, and us, too, to a kind of conversion. To change the way we think, the way we live, the way we understand what God wants of us. The point is clear: change begins within the human heart. That is where the worst aspects of human nature reside—and also the best!

Saturday

To paraphrase Jesus: Nothing you confess would make me love you less.

MY 60-SECOND *Reflection*

....
....
....
....
....
....
....
....
....
....
....
....
....
....
....
....
....

CHALLENGE #3

So if you have been raised with Christ, seek the things that are above, where Christ is, seated at the right hand of God.

Colossians 3:1

IT'S EASY TO SPOT A YELLOW CAR WHEN YOU ARE ALWAYS thinking of a yellow car. It's easy to spot opportunity when you are always thinking of opportunity. It's easy to spot reasons to be angry when you are always feeling anger. You become what you constantly think and feel. Watch yourself. Whenever I get in the mood to purchase a new vehicle or consider getting a new dog, it seems that wherever I go, there it is! Or the breed of dog I want happens to be at the dog park right in front of me. Isn't it incredible what comes into our lives on the basis of where we put our focus? Wouldn't it be interesting if we brought to mind the qualities of Jesus, in a constant way? What do you think would happen? Would the people we meet or see in our daily lives begin to take on the qualities of Jesus? Would we begin to recognize the qualities of Jesus within each person we encounter?

THIS WEEK'S CHALLENGE:
Put your focus on Jesus. Give it a try.
What have you got to lose?

SUNDAY

I once saw a bumper sticker that read, "I'm a veterinarian, therefore I can drive like an animal." That made me realize how many proctologists are on the roads. Now, if our optometrists could help us to see even those proctologist drivers through the loving eyes of God . . .

Monday

Wake up, people. Count your blessings, not your problems.

Tuesday

Dear You:
I think you're awesome. It's all going to work out.
Best wishes,
God

Wednesday

Authenticity always wins. It's your biggest competitive advantage, but maybe you're not using it. You look around at others you perceive to be successful, and you're trying to be them. In reality, if you were more authentically yourself, you'd be more successful.
Be real! Be you!

Thursday

Jesus taught us. Walked with us. Ate with us. Worked with us. Debated with us. And then, after doing nothing wrong, he died for us. We don't deserve it. We didn't earn it. We are all sinners. We are all broken, but we have been given salvation. Thanks be to Jesus for taking up the cross to save us.

Friday

No matter how much pain you might feel right now, in time, you will heal. No matter how lost you might feel, one day, you will find your way. No matter how much darkness might surround your life, you will find your light. No matter how worthless you might believe you are, you will find your purpose. Keep going.

Saturday

Remember, peeps: If you have time to worry, you have time to pray!

....

....

....

....

....

....

....

....

....

....

....

....

....

....

....

....

....

....

....

CHALLENGE #4

Little children, you are from God, and have conquered them

[the false spirits]; *for the one who is in you is greater*

than the one who is in the world. 1 John 4:4

JONAH GETS SWALLOWED BY A WHALE. JOSEPH GETS SOLD INTO slavery by his brothers. The whole nation of Israel wanders the desert. It's easy to have faith when things seem great, as when an angel appears to Mary and says salvation is on the way. But it's harder when things are overwhelming and seem to be going in the wrong direction, as when Jesus gets betrayed by a friend and is sentenced to death.

Choosing to believe that God is up to something good *always* leads to a better day, especially on the days when that's hard to do. Jonah escaped from inside of the whale and saved a whole city. Joseph endured slavery in Egypt and then saved his family from starvation. God fed the nation of Israel in the desert, and they grew closer and more trusting of God. The Virgin gave birth to Jesus, who overcame death in all its forms for me and you. God is always up to something good.

THIS WEEK'S CHALLENGE:
Recognize the good
that God is up to in your life.

SUNDAY

Our culture has accepted two huge lies. First, if you disagree with someone's lifestyle, you must fear or hate them. Second, to love someone means that you agree with everything that person believes and does. Both of these concepts are nonsense. You do not have to compromise your personal convictions to be compassionate.

Monday

No matter how bad my day
is, I know someone is
having a tougher day.
May God bless them.

Tuesday

The cost of being nice, $0. The
cost of being loyal, $0. The cost
of being real, $0. It costs $0 to
be a decent person.

Wednesday

Kindness in words creates
confidence. Kindness in
thinking creates profoundness.
Kindness in giving creates love.

Thursday

When you win, be kind. When
you are ignored, be kind. When
you are stuck, be kind. When
you are upset, be kind. When
you are disappointed, be kind.
When you are in doubt, be
kind. When you are scared,
be kind. Kindness will always
serve you well.

Friday

Thank you, God,
for your grace.
For your mercy.
For your forgiveness.
For your protection.
For your guidance.
For your friendship.
For your peace.
For your unfailing love.
For being my savior.
Amen.

Saturday

Be the reason someone believes in the goodness of people.

....
....
....
....
....
....
....
....
....
....
....
....
....
....
....
....

CHALLENGE #5

Go to the crossroads of the streets, and bring everyone,

the blind, the sick, the righteous and sinners.

All. In the Church there is room for everyone.

—Pope Francis

WHAT DOES IT MEAN TO BE PURE OF HEART? THINK OF PURITY as a glass of water: We know pure water when we see and taste it. It's clean. Bright. Fresh. It tastes good. There are no traces of contamination. And just like with water, impurity can come both from within and without. Crystal-clear spring water that passes through rusty lead pipes is no longer pure. Traveling the journey caused impurity from outside the water to enter in.

Keeping our hearts pure is a matter of where and how we travel through life, as well as how we care for and tend to what is inside of us. Purity can be easy to tap into during church service, but what would it look like to carry that purity of heart into our daily lives? Out to "the crossroads of the streets," as Pope Francis says.

THIS WEEK'S CHALLENGE:
Don't just go to church this week.
Be the Church, too.

SUNDAY

There is no such thing as the ministry of criticism. There is, however, the ministry of encouragement. As it says in Acts 4:36–37, "There was a Levite, a native of Cyprus, Joseph, to whom the apostles gave the name Barnabas (which means 'son of encouragement'). He sold a field that belonged to him, then brought the money, and laid it at the apostles' feet." Find *your* way to encourage others.

Monday

Jesus didn't die so that we would come to church. Jesus did die so that we would become the Church.

Tuesday

Gospel: Jesus often reaches out to sinners even before they ask for forgiveness. It's community first, then conversion. Welcoming, and being welcomed, is transformative.

Wednesday

I can choose to let (_____) define me, confine me, refine me, outshine me . . . or I can choose to move on and leave (_____) behind me.

Thursday

A prayer for today: Following Jesus is a 24/7 lifestyle. May my Christianity be more than giving God an hour every Sunday. May I give of my time to Jesus as freely as he gave of himself for us all. Amen.

Friday

Dear moms, dads, brothers, sisters, sons, daughters, students, teachers, inmates, celebrities, and everyone in between who is battling internal struggles that no one else may even know about: *There. Is. Hope.* And if you're one of the lucky few to not be struggling in such a way, *be* a message of hope for others through your actions.

Saturday

Think about it: Church really happens *outside* of church!

CHALLENGE #6

Conduct yourselves wisely towards outsiders, making the most

of the time. Let your speech always be gracious, seasoned with

salt, so that you may know how you ought to answer everyone.

Colossians 4:5–6

YOUR WORK, YOUR VOCATION, IS EVERY BIT AS MUCH MINISTRY as that of a bishop, priest, or deacon. When we serve others, particularly those who are strangers or poor, overlooked, and undervalued in society, God receives our acts of love as if we were serving him. Jesus says as much in the Gospels. To those who "looked after" Jesus when he was sick, Jesus told them that they would be blessed by the Father. He was asked about this, since these people had never cared for Jesus when he was sick. Jesus answered by explaining that whatever we do for the least of our brothers and sisters, we do for him (Matthew 25:34; 40). Your form of ministry may at times feel like a burden. Today, I hope you also have an appreciation of the dignity and holiness in your call.

THIS WEEK'S CHALLENGE:
Let your actions spread the gospel
more loudly than your words.

New day.

New sunrise.

New morning.

New beginning.

New repentance.

New thanksgivings.

New heart full of love.

New fruit of the Holy Spirit.

New will to do the will of God.

New chance to breathe life
freely.

New flood of God's grace
and mercy.

New message from the
word of God.

Monday

I do not *believe in* miracles;
rather, I *rely on* miracles to get
me through each day!
Think about that.

Tuesday

The gospel is best shared
through example, but if you
spread the Word using your
words, remember that the
gospel is an announcement, not
an argument. You share it, not
shove it.

Wednesday

The disciples couldn't imagine
anything good coming from
a crucifixion. But God's
imagination is so much greater
than ours.

Thursday

It's not your body
or your blood.
It's not your table.
It's not your church.
It's not your invitation.
You are the servant.
You are not the master.
You don't assemble the guest list.
You were appointed an
ambassador of the Good News,
not a bouncer at the door
of Club Heaven.

Friday

When someone, whether
a friend or a stranger, does
something kind for you, *accept*
it. Be grateful and allow the
gesture to instill some type of
compassion within you toward
others.

Saturday

The goal is not to be perfect at the end. The goal is to be better today.

CHALLENGE #6
MY 60-SECOND *Reflection*

CHALLENGE #7

There is no cross, big or small, in our life which

the Lord does not share with us.

—Pope Francis

A LITTLE GIRL WAS AFRAID OF THE DARK. SHE CALLED OUT to her mother, who came to her bedroom and lay down beside her. The mother said, "Honey, you don't ever have to be afraid in the dark. God is always with you." To which the child responded, "I know God is always with me, but I want somebody with skin."

God is with us, yes. It is up to us, as the little girl so sweetly pointed out, to put skin—flesh and bones—on the prayers we pray. Just as Christ—God—was made into flesh at the Incarnation, we as Christ's Church are now the visible, tangible Body of Christ. He wants us to be involved, not just in making petitions and praying prayers, but also in allowing him to bring about the answers to those prayers *through us.* My voice, my compassion, my presence, my energy is called forth because I am a member of the Body of Christ.

> **THIS WEEK'S CHALLENGE:**
> Pray, yes. And as you pray, put skin—flesh and bones—
> on the prayers you make.

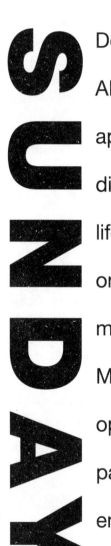

SUNDAY

Dear God:

Allow me to have an appreciation for the different seasons of my life. Some were meant for only a while, but others may be worth revisiting. May I always keep an open mind to the people, passions, and dreams I've encountered along the way. Amen.

Monday

A wise priest once said, "When we die, there will be a reconciliation between who we *think* God is, and who he *actually* is. I'd prefer to get closer to God now, rather than wait until that day."

Tuesday

You know what? Don't wear a cross around your neck if all you're going to do is complain about the one on your back. Think about it!

Wednesday

I used to believe that prayer changes things, but now I know that prayer changes us, and we change things.

Thursday

Hurt people hurt people. That's how pain patterns are passed on from generation to generation. Break the chain today. Meet anger with sympathy, contempt with compassion, cruelty with kindness. Greet grimaces with smiles. Forgive and forget, seeing one another through the eyes of God. Love is the answer.

Friday

It takes six to eight pallbearers to lift you up when you're deceased. Imagine what you could accomplish if you had six to eight people lifting you up while you are living. Pray as if you are one of those people someone else needs to be lifted up—because you are.

Saturday

Don't worry. God is always on time. Trust him.

CHALLENGE #8

"If you love those who love you, what credit is that to you? For even sinners love those who love them. If you do good to those who do good to you, what credit is that to you? For even sinners do the same."

Luke 6:32–33

ONCE WHEN I WAS RIDING IN A TAXI, A CAR SWERVED INTO our lane, forcing my driver to slam on his brakes, skid, and avoid another speeding car by inches. The driver of the swerving car yelled profanities at us. My taxi driver just smiled and waved at the guy.

He explained his reaction: "Many people are like garbage trucks. They run around full of garbage, frustration, anger, and disappointment. As their negativity piles up, they need a place to dump it. Sometimes they dump it on you. I don't take it personally. I just smile, wave, and wish them well."

Successful people don't let garbage take over their day. Life is short, so love the people who treat you right. Pray for the ones who do not—and love them anyway.

THIS WEEK'S CHALLENGE:
Challenge for the whole week, if not your whole life:
Love the unloved.

SUNDAY

Emma, age six, was asked, "What is love?" She replied, "Love is when you're missing some of your teeth, but you're not afraid to smile because you know your friends will still love you even though some of you is missing."

Monday

As a Catholic, my goal is to leave a positive, lasting impact on every person I encounter, whether they chose to follow Jesus or not.

Tuesday

Remember, friends: Don't ask God to guide your footsteps if you're not willing to move your feet.

Wednesday

Your job is not to judge. Your job is not to figure out if someone deserves something. Your job is to help lift the fallen, restore the broken, and heal the hurting.

Thursday

Recall Challenge #1, and then strive to put your name where the word *love* belongs:

Love is patient; love is kind; love is not envious or boastful or arrogant or rude. It does not insist on its own way; it is not irritable or resentful; it does not rejoice in wrongdoing, but rejoices in the truth. It bears all things, believes all things, hopes all things, endures all things.
1 Corinthians 13:4–7

Friday

Father Jim's seven points:

1. God first.
2. Love one another.
3. Never hate.
4. Give generously.
5. Live simply.
6. Forgive quickly.
7. Be kind always.

Saturday

"Let us learn to live with kindness, to love everyone, even when they do not love us." —Pope Francis

MY 60-SECOND *Reflection*

. . . .

. . . .

. . . .

. . . .

. . . .

. . . .

. . . .

. . . .

. . . .

. . . .

. . . .

. . . .

. . . .

. . . .

. . . .

CHALLENGE #9

And be kind to one another, tender-hearted, forgiving one another, as God in Christ has forgiven you. Ephesians 4:32

THERE IS A STORY ABOUT A MAN WHO, WHILE HE LIVED, HAD no particular relationship with God. In fact, he lived quite apart from God, and when he died, he ended up in hell. From his place in hell he managed to get word to a good friend, who came down and stood before the gates of hell. On the other side, his friend stood next to Satan and screamed, "Let him out!" But Satan only laughed, and the iron bars remained closed. The friend went back to earth and managed to coax the man's pastor to try to release him from hell. As the priest stood before the iron gates, he, too, yelled, "Let him out!" Once again, Satan laughed, and the bars stayed in place. Finally, the priest contacted the man's mother, who stood before the gates of hell and forcefully called out, "Let me in!" With that, the doors opened, and her son came forth. It was the mother's love that was liberating. The other two could only consider that the man had to come forth. The mother, however, was willing to stand with him in his torment. Her love found him where he was and freed him from within.

THIS WEEK'S CHALLENGE:
Meet others where they are,
and love without condition.

SUNDAY

We believe in God the Father.

We believe in Jesus Christ.

We believe in the Holy Spirit,
who's given us new life.

We believe in the Crucifixion.

We believe that he conquered
death.

We believe in the Resurrection

—and, he's coming back
again.

Monday

If you don't stick to your values when they're being tested, they're not values; they're hobbies.

Tuesday

Want to find happiness in your life? Appreciate the small stuff. You are blessed more than you realize.

Wednesday

My to-do list for today:
Count my blessings.
Practice kindness.
Let go of what I can't control.
Listen to my heart.
Be productive yet calm.
Just breathe.

Thursday

We might not all be saints with glowing halos, but through consistent acts of kindness, we each can light up the world, one compassionate act at a time.

Friday

Being "pro-life" means defending the lives of the unborn *and* the born. This includes the sick, the poor, the homeless, the aged, the mentally challenged, the inmate, the refugee, the person or people you hate. *All* life. Being pro-life means reverencing *all* human life. Because all life comes from God.

Saturday

In a world where you can be anything, be kind.

MY 60-SECOND *Reflection*

CHALLENGE #10

Be patient, therefore, beloved, until the coming of the LORD.
The farmer waits for the precious crop from the earth, being patient
with it until it receives the early and the late rains. James 5:7

ONE SUNDAY MORNING AT A SMALL SOUTHERN CHURCH, the new pastor called on one of his older deacons to lead the opening prayer. The deacon stood up, bowed his head, and said, "Lord, I hate buttermilk."

The pastor opened one eye and wondered where this was going. The deacon continued, "Lord, I hate lard." Now the pastor was totally perplexed. The deacon concluded, "Lord, I ain't too crazy about plain flour either, but after you mix 'em all together and bake 'em in a hot oven, I just love biscuits."

Lord, help us to realize that when life gets hard, and when things come up that we don't like and we don't understand what you are doing, we need to wait and see what you are making. After you get through mixing and baking, it'll probably be something even better than biscuits. Amen.

THIS WEEK'S CHALLENGE:
When you feel the urge to grow impatient or frustrated, wanting results *now*, pause, breathe, and trust.

SUNDAY

The "Other" Serenity Prayer

God, grant me the serenity

to stop beating myself

up for not doing things

perfectly, the courage to

forgive myself because I'm

working on doing better,

and the wisdom to know

that you already love me

just the way I am. Amen.

Monday

Remember, peeps: The two most important days in your life are the day you are born and the day you find out why.

Tuesday

Knowing is not enough; we must apply. Wishing is not enough; we must do.

Wednesday

Only God can turn a *mess* into a message, a *test* into a testimony, a *trial* into a triumph, a *victim* into a victory.

Thursday

Offering a smile is a simple yet transformative act. It can turn a frown into a halo, and in that instant, we become messengers of God's love.

Friday

Being Christlike doesn't require us to walk on water. It simply means taking steady steps, putting one foot in front of the other, in the direction of faith, love, and compassion.

Saturday

In God's alphabet, *L* comes first: Love, Listen, Learn.

MY 60-SECOND *Reflection*

CHALLENGE #11

Some friends play at friendship but a true friend sticks closer

than one's nearest kin. Proverbs 18:24

MOTHER TERESA'S LEGACY TRANSCENDS CHARITY, AS MARKED by her fearless stance before presidents, governments, and universities when she spoke out against societal injustices. She identified systemic diseases that are eroding humanity, including abortion, callousness, and divisiveness. Her words, which often were met with both accolades and silence, highlighted the root causes of our culture of death. Her profound impact fused charity with social justice. She rallied countless individuals to the work of the Missionaries of Charity while, at the same time, she challenged power holders to confront fundamental issues. Unafraid, she urged us to alter the course of the world by asking the question, "Why do bodies still drift downstream," and then she beckoned us to redirect our efforts *upstream* for true change. What can you do to move your part of the world upstream?

THIS WEEK'S CHALLENGE:
Travel upriver to change the root cause of problems
at the source, before problems occur.

SUNDAY

Jesus shows the power of forgiveness. You must forgive to be forgiven; you must love to be loved. Not everything in life will be "fixed" with justice or revenge, which only spreads and suffocates the world. We will be asked to forgive and love the impossible.

—*Pope Francis*

Monday

Making a million friends is not a miracle. The miracle is to make a friend who will stand with you when millions are against you.

Tuesday

One of the greatest things in life is the realization that we don't know it all. Then we can accept guidance and expertise from others.

Wednesday

God helps.
God heals.
God hears.
God forgives.
God redeems.
God provides.
God cares about you and me.

Thursday

God, without you, I am nothing. All of my life belongs to you alone, and so I ask that you use my life for your glory. Set me apart to do the good works you have planned in advance for me. Change the way I think and the way I live. Draw me closer to you, and remind me of your unfailing love. In Jesus' name. Amen.

Friday

So many messages tell those who are struggling to reach out. Fair enough, but part of what depression does is mute your ability to reach. If you are not depressed and you see someone struggling, *you* reach out. If you notice that someone who used to be around is missing, *you* reach out.

Saturday

Top four rules to leading a great life: Be kind. Be kind. Be kind. Be kind.

....

....

....

....

....

....

....

....

....

....

....

....

....

....

....

....

....

....

....

CHALLENGE #12

"Or how can you say to your neighbor, 'Friend, let me take out the speck in your eye,' when you yourself do not see the log in your own eye? You hypocrite, first take the log out of your own eye, and then you will see clearly to take the speck out of your neighbor's eye."

Luke 6:42

A YOUNG COUPLE MOVES INTO A NEW NEIGHBORHOOD. The next morning while they are eating breakfast, the young woman sees her neighbor hanging the wash outside. "That laundry is not very clean; she doesn't know how to wash correctly. Perhaps she needs better laundry soap." Her husband looks on, remaining silent. Every time her neighbor hangs her wash to dry, the young woman makes the same comments. A month later, the woman is surprised to see a nice clean wash on the line and says to her husband: "Look, she's finally learned how to wash correctly. I wonder who taught her this?" The husband replies, "I got up early this morning and cleaned our windows." And so it is with life: What we see when watching others depends on the clarity of the window through which we look. Before you judge others, take a good look at yourself.

THIS WEEK'S CHALLENGE:
If you begin judging others, don't. Keep your focus on your own garden, not your neighbor's.

SUNDAY

Don't judge. A simple fact of life is that nobody has it easy. Everybody has problems. You never know what people are going through. So before you start judging, criticizing, or mocking others, remember that everybody is fighting their own battle.

Monday

Holy water isn't a detergent, yet it reminds us of the cleansing power of repentance and God's grace.

Tuesday

We're all like stained-glass windows: broken, beautiful, and best viewed with the light shining through.

Wednesday

What are some of the things that were said to you that changed your life for the better? Who said them? A member of your family? A teacher? Friend? Stranger? Multiply those blessings by spreading your own life-altering words of kindness.

Thursday

Charity isn't just for the collection plate. Every kind word, every shared meal, every patient listening ear—that's where we find true charity.

Friday

Being a good Christian doesn't require a halo or wings—just an open heart willing to accept, share, and multiply God's infinite love.

Saturday

God's love is like a parish potluck—there's always more than enough to go around.

. . . .

. . . .

. . . .

. . . .

. . . .

. . . .

. . . .

. . . .

. . . .

. . . .

. . . .

. . . .

. . . .

. . . .

. . . .

. . . .

. . . .

. . . .

CHALLENGE #13

"Blessed are the peacemakers, for they will be called children of God."

Matthew 5:9

The old saying goes "Sticks and stones may break my bones, but words will never hurt me." Really? It has been my experience that this adage could not be more wrong! Physical injuries often heal in time, but the pain from harsh words takes much longer to heal, especially if the words were spoken by someone we love or admire. Often, we do not realize the power of words. What we say can break a person's spirit or confidence. We should ask ourselves: What do my words do? Do they bring comfort and healing, or brokenness and pain? One of the most important things to integrate into our way of speaking is "I am sorry." This simple phrase can carry healing and peace. Do we have the humility to speak those words with sincerity when we've hurt someone? Can we have the humility to accept them when someone offers an apology to us?

THIS WEEK'S CHALLENGE:
Today, let us pray for the grace to recognize the power of our words. May the words we speak bring peace to our troubled world. And may we learn to incorporate "I am sorry" into our everyday lives.

SUNDAY

Many hurt feelings, many lesions in the family begin with the loss of those precious words: "I am sorry." In married life there are many arguments, but I advise you never to let the day end without making peace. And for this, a small gesture is enough.

—*Pope Francis*

Monday

The difference between the right word and the almost-right word is as important as the difference between lightning and a lightning bug.

Tuesday

Sharing joy is like lighting another's candle with your own—neither flame is diminished.

Wednesday

As you go through your day, realize that faith is not the belief that God will do what you want. Faith is the belief that God will align you to do what is right.

Thursday

The saving power of Jesus' sacrifice, every one of his words, every gesture, every look, every feeling, reaches us in the celebration of the sacraments. I am Nicodemus and the Samaritan woman, the possessed man of Capernaum and the paralytic in Peter's house, the sinner who was forgiven, the woman with blood, the daughter of Jairus and the blind man of Jericho, Zacchaeus and Lazarus, and the thief and Peter who were forgiven.

Friday

Mortal: What is a million years like to you?
God: Like one second.
Mortal: What is a million dollars like to you?
God: Like one penny.
Mortal: Can I have a penny?
God: Just a second.

Saturday

Forgive your enemies. It messes with their minds.

CHALLENGE #14

Jesus chose Peter and Paul despite their sins. The LORD does not work miracles with those who consider themselves righteous, but with those who know themselves needy. —Pope Francis

---

ST. PETER WOULDN'T HAVE BEEN MY FIRST PICK AS A DISCIPLE. He was not the most prayerful, or the smartest. He probably smelled of fish, and he was quick to speak when he should have left well enough alone. Nope, I wouldn't have picked him. Good thing Jesus didn't ask my opinion. He knew Peter's sinfulness and brokenness, and he knew that Peter would deny him. But he knew what was possible with Peter. Of course, he was right. Eventually, Peter the sinner became Peter the saint.

You and I are like Peter. Despite our brokenness, despite our sinfulness, we have been chosen by God to be his hands, his feet, his messengers of mercy. He knows our hearts better than we do, and he knows what is possible when we "cast our nets" and trust in him. We can hide behind excuses that keep us from reaching our full potential, or we can be like Peter, who, with God's grace and mercy and love, became a saint.

THIS WEEK'S CHALLENGE:
Recognize how we are God's messengers of mercy
in our everyday lives.

SUNDAY

A kind gesture is a visible sign of God's love working through us, transforming our simple actions into a powerful testament of his mercy, affecting lives in profound and lasting ways.

Monday

I have given God a million reasons not to love me. None of them changed his mind.

Tuesday

I asked God, "Why do you continue to bless me?" He replied, "So you can continue to be a blessing to the people around you."

Wednesday

You see worthless. God sees priceless. You see pain, but God sees a purpose. You see unworthy and undeserving, but God sees you through eyes of mercy.

Thursday

Even when life is puzzling, every piece of kindness you give to others helps complete their puzzle of life.

Friday

Seven Cardinal Rules of Life

1. Make peace with your past so it doesn't spoil your present.
2. What other people think about you is none of your business.
3. Time heals almost everything; give time some time.
4. No one is in charge of your happiness except you.
5. Don't compare your life to others'.
6. Stop thinking too much.
7. Smile. After all, you don't own all the problems in the world.

Saturday

Look back and thank God. Look forward and trust God. Look around and serve God. Look within and find God.

MY 60-SECOND *Reflection*

....
....
....
....
....
....
....
....
....
....
....
....
....
....
....
....
....
....
....
....

CHALLENGE #15

I lift up my eyes to the hills—from where will my help come?

My help comes from the LORD, who made heaven and earth.

Psalm 121:1–4

SOME TRADITIONS REFER TO PSALM 121 AS THE "TRAVELER'S psalm." It is sometimes used as a reminder of God's careful protection as he accompanies us along the paths of life. Coming and going. Beginning our days. As we engage in our work or as we care for others and ourselves. When we return home after a long day's toil. In the valleys and on the mountaintops, literal and figurative. In the journey of our lives, God promises to be with us and to help us.

This same psalm continues with a reminder that God walks with us not only as companion but also as provider and protector, always on call, always there. *"He will not let your foot be moved; he who keeps you will not slumber"* (Psalm 121:3). God doesn't take coffee breaks. He's got your back.

THIS WEEK'S CHALLENGE:
Consider all the times when God has had your back,
and, together, you have persevered.

SUNDAY

This recently occurred to me: If I spent as much time with my Bible as I do with my smartphone, I'd be a better person and priest. Let's put the phones on silent more often, then turn up the volume for God.

Monday

To care for those who once cared for us is one of life's highest honors.

Tuesday

Be careful when you blindly follow the masses. Sometimes the *m* in *masses* is silent. Follow the Lord instead!

Wednesday

It's important to realize that believing in God does not protect you from unexplained tragedy. Your faith provides a foundation to deal with it. God is with you, always.

Thursday

We are all ordinary. We are all spectacular. We are all boring. We are all bold. We are all helpless. We are all heroes. It just depends on the day. Be kind to yourself on the trying days and remain humble on the triumphant days.

Friday

Follow your heart, not your mind. Slow down your racing thoughts and tune in to the feelings of your heart and your innermost self. The heart that is sound and informed is the voice of God speaking intimately and directly!

Saturday

Incarnation is mercy, and mercy is incarnation. Think about it!

MY 60-SECOND *Reflection*

....

....

....

....

....

....

....

....

....

....

....

....

....

....

....

....

CHALLENGE #16

You show that you are a letter of Christ, prepared by us, written not with ink but with the Spirit of the living God, not on tablets of stone but on tablets of human hearts. 2 Corinthians 3:3

GOD CALLS ALL KINDS OF PEOPLE TO ALL KINDS OF VOCATIONS. But our culture sometimes forgets that *all* work accomplished in the course of faithfully living out our calling from God is ministry. When husbands and wives build and share love in their homes, that is ministry. When lawyers protect the rights of their clients, that is ministry. And when you fulfill your day's work, whatever your occupation or life's calling may be, that is ministry. These things are absolutely every bit as much ministry as what my brother priests and I do inside, in the church, as well as outside, in the Church.

All occupations don't pay the same or come with the same struggles and rewards. But all vocations are holy ministry that emanates from God's heart and enters the world through you to care for God's people. And that means that what you do every day has its origin in the heart of God and his love for you and his people.

THIS WEEK'S CHALLENGE:
May your vocation be your ministry, and may your work fulfill God's purpose for your life.

SUNDAY

This day's reminders:

It's a new day.

You are forgiven.

You are loved.

You can make a difference today.

You can make a difference every day.

You are worth it.

God has a plan.

Trust in God's plan.

Enjoy.

Monday

Without dreams, we reach nothing. Without love, we feel nothing. And without God, we are nothing.

Tuesday

Remember: God's not looking at your ability, he's looking at your availability! How will you show up today and every day? How will you answer God's calling?

Wednesday

Everyone wishes their life came with instructions, but it already has them—in the Bible.

Thursday

Regardless of your vocation, if you keep food in the fridge, clothes in the closet, have a bed to sleep on and a roof over your head, you are richer than billions of people on Earth. Appreciate what you have!

Friday

Good things come to those who wait. Greater things come to those who get out there and do what it takes to make those things happen. Roll up your sleeves, lace up your work boots, and get to it!

Saturday

Avoid stress. Deal with things as they are, not as you think they should be.

MY 60-SECOND *Reflection*

CHALLENGE #17

"Pray then in this way: Our Father in heaven, hallowed be your name. Your kingdom come. Your will be done, on earth as it is in heaven. Give us this day our daily bread. And forgive us our debts, as we also have forgiven our debtors. And do not bring us to the time of trial, but rescue us from the evil one." Matthew 6:9–13

IN THOSE FEW WORDS OF THE OUR FATHER, JESUS TAUGHT US how to pray. We don't need a theology degree, fancy words, a special place, or long periods of quiet introspection to pray. All that's necessary is to begin. To reach out to God wherever we may be with simplicity, with intimacy, and with the heart of a child.

When we lift the simple words of the Our Father from our souls up to God, we accomplish so much. We unite ourselves to all God's children. Yes, God is my Father. Yes, he is your Father. But Jesus taught us to pray by saying *our* Father. May everyone you encounter today be included in your prayer to be *our* prayer.

THIS WEEK'S CHALLENGE:
As you encounter people in your daily life, see them as part of one family, *our* family, because we are all children of God.

Judas had:

The best leader.

The best master.

The best teacher.

The best friend.

And he still failed.

The problem was not Jesus.

The problem was that

Judas put his faith in others

and in himself rather than

in Jesus.

Monday

If you have the power to make someone happy, do it. The world needs more of that.

Tuesday

Only three words: *Love more today.*

If those three words didn't sink in the first time, here they are again: *Love. More. Today.*

Wednesday

Through the Eucharist, we receive a gift. We take into our hands and onto our tongues something that is astounding: We are being given God.

Thursday

Nations often remove controversial statues in the name of progress, love, and equality for all, but until we as a human race figure out how to remove the hate in people's hearts, nothing will change. If you want to change the world, start with your own heart. It may not change the world, but it will certainly change *your* world.

Friday

God's mercy is like a sunrise— every morning, it lights up our world, bringing warmth and the promise of a fresh start.

Saturday

A faith incapable of showing mercy to others isn't faith. It's just an ideology. —Pope Francis

MY 60-SECOND *Reflection*

CHALLENGE #18

Then he began to speak, and taught them, saying:

"Blessed are the poor in spirit, for theirs is the kingdom of heaven."

Matthew 5:2–3

ONE OF THE MOST RECOGNIZABLE PASSAGES FROM THE GOSPELS is referred to as the Beatitudes, a series of pronouncements that Jesus offers as a way of living life. Each of the Beatitudes begins with the phrase "Blessed are . . ." and then Jesus names the reward or blessing people who live their lives in accordance with this teaching will receive.

Although it may sound like a Sunday school cliché, the blessings are realized by an attitude, or way of being, as we go about life, work, and relationships. A "be attitude." Perhaps the takeaway for this week is just this: holiness may come less from what we do and perhaps more from *how* we do. From how we go about life and work.

This week, be blessed as you are a blessing.

I will be praying for you.

THIS WEEK'S CHALLENGE:
Notice all the ways you are blessed,
especially the small ways.

SUNDAY

None of us must feel "superior" to anyone. None of us should look down at others from above. The only time we can look at a person in this way is when we are helping them to stand up.

—*Pope Francis*

Monday

Better to stand with God and be judged by the world than to stand with the world and be judged by God.

Tuesday

When evil and hate crucified our Lord Jesus Christ, he still rose powerfully from the grave with love. When faced with hate, you can rise with love too. Except you don't have to rise from the grave—probably just from the couch!

Wednesday

In a society that has you counting money, pounds, calories, and steps, be a rebel and count your blessings.

Thursday

When "The Word" is considered good news to the oppressive but bad news to the oppressed, then it no longer resembles the gospel of our Lord Jesus Christ.

Friday

Once shaken, we can be broken. Only then can we be remade more perfectly into Christ's image. The formula goes like this: shake, break, remake. Do not be discouraged if you're in a period of shaking or even breaking in your life. Trust in God and you will be made whole.

Saturday

All your life you will be faced with a choice. You can choose love or hate. I choose love. —Johnny Cash

CHALLENGE #19

The LORD is your keeper; the LORD is your shade at your right hand.

The sun shall not strike you by day, nor the moon by night.

The LORD will keep you from all evil; he will keep your life.

The LORD will keep your going out and your coming in

from this time on and forevermore.

Psalm 121:5–8

AS CHILDREN WE OFTEN WANT TO ASSERT OUR INDEPENDENCE, saying, in effect, we don't need a "keeper." But as adults, and especially when we are pressed to our limits, the idea of someone looking out for us can be a comfort. It is true, yes, we can be our brothers' and our sisters' keepers, especially during trying times, but, as we are reminded in the psalm, God is there to "keep" us, too. To keep us safe, to help us feel less alone, and to encourage and strengthen us.

May you feel the closeness of that protection as God keeps you, walking near you, and walking with you.

THIS WEEK'S CHALLENGE:
Reflect on the ways God has always protected you
and will always keep you.

SUNDAY

As our keeper, God knows what lies ahead of us. When one door seems to close, trust in God's plan for your life. Sometimes, he's gently redirecting our steps toward a door that leads us closer to fulfilling our purpose.

Monday

Each day is a divine gift, a chance to reflect God's love, to grow in faith, and to inspire those around us.

Tuesday

Challenges? Think of them as life's hands-on training sessions. With each new obstacle handled, we become a stronger, more resilient version of ourselves.

Wednesday

A genuine smile, a kind word, or a moment of understanding can radically change someone's day. Make the extra effort to be that change.

Thursday

There's a reassuring calm in knowing that no matter how challenging life may be, God is our keeper, walking with us through every storm, turning every obstacle into a stepping stone, and guiding us with his mercy and grace.

Friday

Think of compassion as an endless well. The more you share, the more it is replenished. From a kind word to a helping hand, every gesture, no matter how subtle, can make a significant difference in our own lives and in the lives of those we encounter.

Saturday

The love and positivity you radiate today can become tomorrow's beacon of hope for someone else.

CHALLENGE #20

"For God so loved the world that he gave his only Son,

so that everyone who believes in him may not perish

but may have eternal life." John 3:16

ULTIMATELY, IT ALL COMES DOWN TO THIS ONE SINGLE, BASIC, profound truth: You are loved. It's so simple to say, but sometimes it can be a hard thing to understand. We need to let this truth penetrate deep enough into the heart that it guides how we approach life and work and family and all the rest. *You are loved.* Isn't the whole story of humanity's relationship with God really a series of amazing episodes on that theme? God loves us. God loves you. And oh, my friend, what lengths God will go to so that we can understand and live in the beauty of this truth!

Give yourself five minutes to think of nothing else but this wonderful truth: God knows you, and God loves you.

THIS WEEK'S CHALLENGE:
Extend those sixty seconds. Dedicate five minutes each day to notice and reflect on the many ways you are known and loved by God.

SUNDAY

Keep in mind that it only
takes a second to say:

I love you.

I'm sorry.

Can we talk?

You were right.

I don't want to be at odds
with you.

Stop letting pride and ego
hold you back from
happiness and meaningful
connections in life.

If you think about it, God
gave himself to you; give
yourself to God. Enough
said. Period.

Monday

Reminder for the day: I am too blessed to be stressed and I am too anointed to be disappointed.

Tuesday

Good Rules to Live By:
Pray unceasingly.
Be thankful for everything.
Be kind.
Be strong.
Stay confident.
Remain humble.
And always give God the glory.

Wednesday

Kindness is prayer in action. Pay attention to how many times and in how many different ways you can be kind today.

Thursday

Don't forget: the same God who forgave Moses the murderer, Rahab the prostitute, David the adulterer, Peter the denier, and Paul the Christian persecutor can also forgive you. No one is beyond God's mercy. We all are welcome to God's grace.

Friday

Isaiah 41:10: read it.
It's meant for you. To refresh your memory, it reads:

*Do not fear, for I am with you;
do not be afraid, for I am your
God; I will strengthen you, I will
help you, I will uphold you with
my victorious right hand.*

Saturday

If we really want to love, we must learn how to forgive.
—Mother Teresa

MY 60-SECOND *Reflection*

CHALLENGE #21

So we, who are many, are one body in Christ, and individually we
are members one of another. Romans 12:5

SET IN A RUN-OF-THE-MILL NEIGHBORHOOD DIVE, *CHEERS* was an immensely popular television program in the 1980s that showed the same people stopping by the bar for a drink and camaraderie. The theme song captured the beauty of that simple concept: "You wanna go where everybody knows your name." Isn't there something special about walking into a room—whether an office, the gym, or even a bar—where everyone knows you? And maybe more important, where you feel like you belong?

Belonging is where being special and unique in yourself comes together with being a part of a great and expansive "us." Part of the reality that God gives to each one of us is that we *all* belong. We all belong with God. And we all belong with one another. Whatever separates, divides, categorizes, or labels us is far less important than our belonging. Yes, you belong.

THIS WEEK'S CHALLENGE:
Reach out. Make that phone call. Send that text.
Share in moments of belonging
and invite others to feel welcome.

SUNDAY

Sometimes our lives can feel like a television series—there's always another episode, and we never know what's going to happen. But remember: God's got the remote. We're in good hands.

Monday

Jesus had a public ministry, public death. Nothing hidden. Don't be a hidden Christian. Our world needs you to be a very public witness.

Tuesday

In today's culture, being Christlike is like going viral, but instead of likes and shares, we aim for love and care.

Wednesday

Baptized in God's love, we are called to be living sacraments— visible signs of his divine mercy in the world.

Thursday

You don't need a theology degree to love your neighbor, just a heart ready to embrace and hands willing to help. Acts of love transcend all barriers and bind us together.

Friday

When we serve others, we are serving God. Every helping hand is an extension of his love, every comforting word a whisper of his grace. This is our divine calling: to be God's love in action.

Saturday

Prayers are like God's voicemail. Trust me, he never misses a message.

CHALLENGE #22

While he was saying this, a cloud came and overshadowed them;

and they were terrified as they entered the cloud. Then from the cloud

came a voice that said, 'This is my Son, my Chosen; listen to him!'

When the voice had spoken, Jesus was found alone. And they kept

silent and in those days told no one any of the things they had seen.

Luke 9:34–36

TWO FRIENDS WALKED DOWN FIFTH AVENUE IN MANHATTAN carrying on a conversation. It was difficult because it was the busiest time of day, with the rumbling of the engines of buses, cars, and trucks, horns blaring, and crowds of noisy pedestrians. One friend stopped and asked, "Do you hear that cricket chirping?" The other replied, "With all this racket, you mean to tell me you can hear a cricket chirping?" "Yes, I can. Now watch this." He took a handful of fifty-cent pieces from his pocket and threw them into the air. When the coins clinked on the concrete sidewalk, everyone within earshot stopped walking to search for the money.

The first friend said, "In life, you hear what you're listening for."

> **THIS WEEK'S CHALLENGE:**
> *Listen—*
> for the voice of God in your life.

Jesus is my Way.

Jesus is my King.

Jesus is my Lord.

Jesus is my Truth.

Jesus is my Savior.

Jesus is my Healer.

Jesus is my Brother.

Jesus is my Master.

Jesus is my Teacher.

Jesus is my Deliverer.

Jesus is my Shepherd.

Jesus is my everything.

Monday

God designed me,
created me,
blesses me,
teaches me,
supports me,
defends me,
protects me,
forgives me,
heals me,
loves me.

Tuesday

As I tell people all across the globe, if you can't be positive, at least be quiet!

Wednesday

Words of mercy and encouragement today: Never let anyone tell you that you can't do something, because the Bible says you can do all things through God who strengthens you.

Thursday

Seven big influences on who you will become:

1. How you pray
2. What you watch
3. What you read
4. What you listen to
5. Who you spend your time with
6. The things you say to yourself
7. The thoughts you choose to accept as true

Friday

If you didn't hear it with your own ears or see it with your own eyes, don't invent it with your small mind and share it with your big mouth.

Saturday

When in doubt, say nothing. Truth matters.

MY 60-SECOND *Reflection*

CHALLENGE #23

See what love the Father has given us, that we should be called

children of God; and that is what we are. 1 John 3:1

A WOMAN ONCE SHARED WITH ME: "I JUST FEEL LIKE ANOTHER one in the crowd, to my family, to my friends, at work . . . to God. Just another data point. Is that all we are?" What she said next pricked my heart so much it became a part of my prayers for some time thereafter, and stirred in me a host of reflections. She said, "I just wonder if I'll ever do or accomplish enough to matter." Maybe you've never wondered that. What a gift if that's true for you! Please pray for people like this woman who question their worth.

The wonderful truth is that the answer is no. No, we can't ever do or accomplish enough. It's just not possible. We don't have that kind of ability or power. But that is where the beauty of God's love shines so bright. That's because being special, belonging, and being loved aren't about anything we do. Rather, they are who we are and, more precisely, who God is. You, my friend, are created in the image and likeness of God, and that is enough. You *are* enough.

THIS WEEK'S CHALLENGE:
Reflect on all the ways you are created in the image
and likeness of God.

SUNDAY

A baby mosquito came back after his first time flying. His dad asked, "How do you feel?" The little one replied, "It was wonderful. Everywhere I went people were waving their hands and clapping for me!"

Attitude changes life. So why not change yours? Choose happiness.

Monday

Prayer isn't to remind God
what your problems are;
prayer is to remind your
problems who God is.

Tuesday

God is for the sinners.
For the hopeless.
For the broken.
For the ones who don't know
that God loves them.
Bring your love to life
inside of them.

Wednesday

The Gospel says that between
the time the risen Christ
appeared to Mary and the time
she announced his resurrection
to the disciples, she was the
Church. Go then and, like Mary,
be the Church, for you may be
the only church people attend.

Thursday

Trust me: Nobody is as
successful as social media makes
them appear to be, and nobody
is as good-looking as filters make
them seem. The only worthwhile
comparison to make is who you
were yesterday and who you are
today. Focus on that.

Friday

May God remember you like
Noah.
May God protect you like
Daniel.
May God heal you like Moses.
May God prosper you like
Isaac.
May God anoint you like
David.
May God answer you like
Elijah.
May God use you like Paul.
May God intervene for you like
Esther.
In Jesus' name. Amen.

Saturday

Who saw Jesus in you today?

....
....
....
....
....
....
....
....
....
....
....
....
....
....
....
....
....
....

CHALLENGE #24

For whatever is born of God conquers the world. And this is the victory that conquers the world, our faith. 1 John 5:4

IN ONE OF THE MOST NOTABLE MOMENTS IN SPORTS HISTORY, a Kenyan runner was just a few feet from the finish line but became confused with the signage and stopped running, thinking he had completed the race. A Spanish athlete was right behind him and after realizing what was happening, he started shouting at the Kenyan for him to continue running, but the Kenyan didn't understand him. The Spanish athlete eventually caught up to him and instead of passing him, he pushed him to victory.

A journalist later asked the Spanish athlete, "Why did you do that?" The athlete replied, "My dream is that someday we can have a kind of community where we push and help each other to win." The journalist insisted, "But why did you let the Kenyan win?" The athlete replied, "I didn't let him win. He was going to win." The journalist insisted again, "But you could have won!" The athlete looked at him and replied, "But what would be the merit of my victory? What would be the honor in that medal? What would my mom think of that?"

THIS WEEK'S CHALLENGE:
Let us reflect on how we're choosing to win. What values are we passing on to our families and to others?

SUNDAY

I'm American and I'm Catholic, but if I emphasize any distinctions between these things, I set myself apart from and raise barriers to other people. The better thing to do is pay more attention to the ways I am similar to others.

Monday

A thought for reflection: People lose their way when they lose their why.

Tuesday

Before you preach to me about your passion for your faith, teach me about your faith through your compassion for your neighbors.

Wednesday

Be brave. Be strong. Don't give up. Expect God.

As Psalm 31:24 reminds us: *Be strong, and let your heart take courage, all you who wait for the LORD.*

Thursday

Real success comes from these things:

1. Humility
2. Hard work
3. Trust in God
4. Gratitude
5. Serving others
6. Prayer
7. Good coffee, wine, bourbon, or vodka

You need 1–6 every day to hit your goals. You may need 7 to help you enjoy them. Life isn't all about work; it's also about joy!

Friday

If you have the chance to make people happy, just do it. Sometimes people struggle silently in ways we will never know. Maybe your act of kindness can make their day.

Saturday

When we lose God, it is not God who is lost.

MY 60-SECOND *Reflection*

CHALLENGE #25

If any of you is lacking in wisdom, ask God, who gives to all generously and ungrudgingly, and it will be given you. James 1:5

SELF-SUFFICIENCY. RELYING ON OUR OWN WISDOM, KNOWLEDGE, expertise. Being the source of our own accomplishments and success. These are held as important values in the predominant culture, and they are good values. Furthermore, we all have our part to play in finding and cultivating the good in the world around us. But do you alone ultimately determine the measures of success? The wisdom here is to not lean or rely completely on your own understanding or expertise or skill, but to also intentionally make room for God's understanding, God's perspective, God's love, so that it can work in this world through you. And that is a process that very often goes beyond our understanding.

If there are parts of your day or week (or month or year) when trusting is difficult or peace is hard to find, see if there's a way to make a little more room for God. God will show up, and you will be blessed.

THIS WEEK'S CHALLENGE:
How can you make room for God's understanding along with your own?

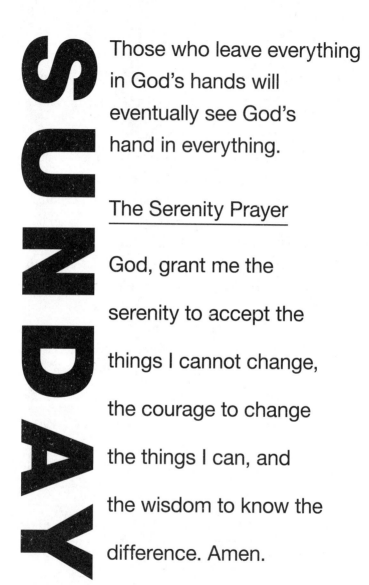

SUNDAY

Those who leave everything in God's hands will eventually see God's hand in everything.

The Serenity Prayer

God, grant me the serenity to accept the things I cannot change, the courage to change the things I can, and the wisdom to know the difference. Amen.

Monday

Regret looks back. Fear looks around. Worry looks in. Faith looks up. Trust in the Lord always.

Tuesday

When life gives you a hundred reasons to cry, show life that you have a thousand reasons to smile.

Wednesday

Many a person who planned on getting saved at the eleventh hour died at ten-thirty. None of us knows how much time we have.

Thursday

Peter: Nobody can save everybody.
Jesus: Hold my wine.

Friday

Twelve steps to self-care:

1. If it feels wrong, don't do it.
2. Say exactly what you mean.
3. Don't be a people pleaser.
4. Trust your instincts.
5. Never speak badly about yourself.
6. Never give up on your dreams.
7. Don't be afraid to say no.
8. Don't be afraid to say yes.
9. Be kind to yourself.
10. Let go of what you can't control.
11. Stay away from drama and negativity.
12. *Love.*

Saturday

Give God your anxiety. It doesn't stress him out.

MY 60-SECOND *Reflection*

CHALLENGE #26

"Blessed are those who hunger and thirst for righteousness,

for they will be filled." Matthew 5:6

JESUS PAINTS WHAT SEEM TO BE DICHOTOMIES THROUGHOUT the "be-attitudes." Perhaps this helps us understand what it means to be blessed. Jesus says that the poor, the meek, and those who hunger for righteousness are those who are—not *will be*, but *are*—blessed. When Jesus directs his attention to the righteous, or those who believed themselves to be righteous, he almost always condemns them. Somehow, they veered off course. They lost, among other things, their humility. They stopped hungering for righteousness.

For Socrates, acknowledging what one doesn't know is a true sign of wisdom. Another sign of wisdom is recognizing our frailty and imperfection in a way that makes us hunger for holiness, and holiness is at the core of what it means to be righteous and blessed. In your hunger, Jesus promises that you will be fed. You will be blessed.

THIS WEEK'S CHALLENGE:
Do you hunger for righteousness?
What are you doing to satisfy that hunger?

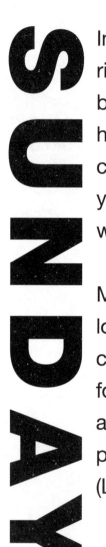

In your hunger for righteousness, may you be blessed this week. In your hunger, may you provide comfort to others, and may you be comforted by the word of the Lord. Amen.

My Father . . .
loves me (John 3:16),
cares for me (Matthew 6:26),
forgives me (Psalm 103:12),
and
persistently pursues me (Luke 19:10).

Monday

The fact that our heart yearns for something Earth can't supply is proof to me that heaven must be our home.

Tuesday

If you have a Bible, read it. If you read the Bible, believe it. If you believe the Bible, live it.

Wednesday

Sometimes we must take a good look in the mirror and recognize that if we're not hungry for Christ, we're probably too full of ourselves.

Thursday

Heal me, Lord, and I will be healed. Save me and I will be saved. For you are the one I praise. In Jesus' name I pray. Amen.

Friday

God has a habit of picking up nobodies and making them somebodies. God lifts us up when we make room for him in our lives—not when we believe ourselves to be righteous, but when we long for his presence—the presence that makes us whole.

Saturday

It's not a religion. It's a relationship.

MY 60-SECOND *Reflection*

....

....

....

....

....

....

....

....

....

....

....

....

....

....

....

....

....

....

....

....

CHALLENGE #27

The angel said to her, "Do not be afraid, Mary, for you have found favor with God. And now, you will conceive in your womb and bear a son, and you will name him Jesus." Luke 1:30–31

HAVE YOU EVER JUST PUSHED "PAUSE" ON EVERYTHING THAT seems like it must get done *right now* so that you can visit a family member you haven't seen for a while, or call someone who needs cheering up? I'm amazed at how what seems a selfless gesture on my part never fails to leave *me* feeling encouraged, uplifted, and energized!

Right after Mary gets the news that changed everything she was planning for the future, God asks her to go visiting. How could visiting Elizabeth, an expectant relative, be important with all that was about to happen? But something wonderful happens during that visit. The two unborn cousins, Jesus and John the Baptist, recognize each other in the womb, and the two women become a blessing to each other. Sometimes our encounter with God happens when we pause what seems to be so pressing and simply go visiting.

THIS WEEK'S CHALLENGE:
What in your life can you pause
so that you can "go visiting" instead?

SUNDAY

It's Sunday.

I'm free.

I'm alive.

I'm loved.

I'm saved.

I'm blessed. I'm forgiven.

I'm restored. I'm redeemed.

I'm remade. I'm fearless.

I'm important.

I'm cherished.

God is good—all the time.

106

Monday

I'd rather attend a church with messed-up people who love God than religious people who dislike messed-up people.

Tuesday

Yes, Christ suffered on the cross. But remember, in life he also danced, sang, and rejoiced. Embrace joy!

Wednesday

Do you sin? God forgives. Do you worry? God's in control. Are you empty? God restores. Are you alone? God is with you.

Thursday

There's always some truth behind saying, "Just kidding."

There's always some knowledge behind saying, "I don't know."

There's always some emotion behind saying, "I don't care."

And there's always some pain behind saying, "I'm okay."

Pay attention, and learn to love and support one another better.

Friday

Let your goal for today be to reach out. Make that phone call to a friend or family member you haven't spoken to for some time. Spread a little kindness to someone who needs it. Being nice is contagious. Pass it on.

Saturday

I am realistic—I expect miracles.

MY 60-SECOND *Reflection*

CHALLENGE #28

For in the one Spirit we were all baptized into one body—Jews or

Greeks, slaves or free—and we were all made to drink of one Spirit.

1 Corinthians 12:13

EVER HEARD ABOUT THE TEXAN WHO BOUGHT TEN ADJOINING ranches in Texas and branded them all together under one name? When asked what he called the mega ranch, he rattled off, "Double R Bar, Crooked Creek, Broken Arrow, Winding Brook, and more . . ."

Astounded at the thought of this vast ranch, the friend said, "You must have an unbelievable number of cattle on your mega ranch." The Texan replied, "Well, actually, no. Not many of them survived the branding."

We are "branded" as Americans, Catholics, and so many other labels in our lives. It's up to us to see through those labels and recognize that there is only one label that gives us life: children of God.

> **THIS WEEK'S CHALLENGE:**
> Blur the lines of division in your heart
> that separate you from others.

SUNDAY

I challenge everyone reading this book to go twenty-four hours without complaining about anything. There are millions of people in this world who would trade places with you, no matter how bad you think things are. Keep everything in perspective.

Monday

Being kind doesn't have a price tag. So make sure that your kindness is never in short supply.

Tuesday

The gospel says that young or old, Black or white, rich or poor, gay or straight, you are a member of God's family. Don't let anyone tell you otherwise.

Wednesday

Racism is stupid. It's an insult to God because it arrogantly implies that God goofed up when he chose to make us different. Nonidentical. Uniquely beautiful.

Thursday

Your priestly prescription for today is to say the following words with me, and welcome them into your heart and mind: *Hate has no home here.* And repeat it again. *Hate has no home here.* Repeat those words as often as necessary to achieve your desired results of a heart that hate cannot call home.

Friday

I refuse to hate people because of their vocation.

I refuse to hate people because of their race.

I refuse to hate people because of their sexual orientation.

I refuse to hate people.

I refuse to hate.

Saturday

Who am I to judge another when I myself walk imperfectly?

MY 60-SECOND *Reflection*

CHALLENGE #29

"Are not two sparrows sold for a penny? Yet not one of them will fall to the ground unperceived by your Father. And even the hairs of your head are all counted. So do not be afraid; you are of more value than many sparrows." Matthew 10:29–31

YES, YOU ARE SPECIAL. UNIQUE. A ONE-OF-A-KIND PERSON. And yet at the same time, you are part of the entire human family. In God's infinite love and goodness, being part of the human family doesn't diminish the ways you are special and loved by God. It doesn't diminish anything about you. In fact, it expands on who you are because you are never alone.

Think of the child on the playground whose heart hurts because she is left out of the game. Think of the adult who doesn't feel included by his colleagues. The fear and hurt can feel very similar. As we live life embracing our uniqueness and our "part of"-ness together, something changes. What's one way this lifts you up today? What's one way it invites you to lift someone else up?

THIS WEEK'S CHALLENGE:
Be a source of encouragement—for others
and for yourself.

SUNDAY

It's good to expect miracles, but it's unreasonable to expect them to happen by your design. Trust in God's divine timing for your life and know that God's plans for you are far greater than anything you can conceive.

Monday

We are not all in the same boat. But we are all in the same storm. Support others. Don't judge. Be kind.

Tuesday

Catholics and Christians, remember that you are a walking, talking advertisement for the kingdom of God. Don't tarnish the brand!

Wednesday

"Miracles are a retelling in small letters of the very same story which is written across the whole world in letters too large for some of us to see."
—C.S. Lewis

Thursday

It's been my experience that the world will shake you, rate you, and try to break you. But let me tell you, having God on your side is what makes you. Always remember that God made you to withstand anything the world might throw at you, because God, as your Creator, can and will remake you.

Friday

Consider this: Jesus endured beatings, humiliation, betrayal, and even death on the cross. Yet against all odds, he rose from the dead. No matter what you're going through, remember that you too can rise above any obstacles you face. He died so that you may live!

Saturday

Never forget how wildly capable you are.

....

....

....

....

....

....

....

....

....

....

....

....

....

....

....

....

....

CHALLENGE #30

For the mountains may depart and the hills be removed, but my

steadfast love shall not depart from you, and my covenant of peace

shall not be removed, says the LORD, who has compassion on you.

Isaiah 54:10

IT IS HARD TO CULTIVATE A PATTERN OF PRAYER WHEN YOUR days are as full as they so often are, rushing around from dawn until dusk. Even so, we deeply desire a more vibrant life of prayer amid the busyness.

There is a simple but powerful way to delve deeper into prayer: Create a prayer routine in the beginning, middle, and end of your day. Morning, noon, and night, or whatever something similar looks like with your schedule. When your feet first touch the floor in the morning, at the first taste of your midday meal or coffee, and when you lay your head on the pillow at night, for example. It doesn't take anything special to practice giving these moments to God, which in turn will mark your whole day for and with the God who loves you.

THIS WEEK'S CHALLENGE:
Delve deeper by routinely praying throughout your day, every morning, midday, and night.

SUNDAY

There comes a pivotal moment in your life when your focus shifts. Suddenly, it's no longer about asking, "God, what can you do for me?" Instead, you find yourself asking, "Lord, what can I do for you?" Embracing this transition is where true purpose and fulfillment reside.

Monday

Never beg for a seat when you can build your own table. Read that twice.

Tuesday

What I have learned is that when people say they'd like to be in your shoes, they're usually saying that after the difficult journey is finished.

Wednesday

There will be haters.

There will be doubters.

There will be nonbelievers.

Then there will be *you* proving them wrong!

Thursday

Consider this: Self-esteem shouldn't hinge on the opinions of others. What truly matters is how you perceive yourself. After all, it's called *self*-esteem, not *their*-esteem! Don't let others define your worth or value. Embrace your uniqueness and be confident in who you are.

Friday

Have you ever felt worthless or unloved? Well, my friend, let me introduce you to someone who thinks you're absolutely priceless—Jesus Christ himself! He loves you unconditionally and is always there for you, ready to embrace you with open arms.

Saturday

No mess is too messy for the grace of Jesus.

MY 60-SECOND *Reflection*

CHALLENGE #31

A glad heart makes a cheerful countenance, but by sorrow of heart the spirit is broken. Proverbs 15:13

MOTHER TERESA IS SAID TO HAVE REMARKED, "WE SHALL never know all the good that a simple smile can do." One of Mother Teresa's lasting legacies is the beauty of her smile. The most common images of her often include hands held together in a prayerful manner, along with the radiance and glow of a smile bursting from the depths of sorrow and joy mingled together. It seems as if her smile was an essential, intentional, mindful, heartfelt part of her mission and ministry.

Offering a smile might have ripple effects beyond what you could ever imagine. Like Mother Teresa, you, too, can be an ambassador of light. Don't forget to look for the smiles on the faces around you. Give yourself the gift of plugging into that profound channel of light and grace. You'll never know all the good your smile will accomplish, and you might be pleasantly surprised at what goodness the smiles of others can work in your heart.

THIS WEEK'S CHALLENGE:
Give and receive smiles
in abundance.

SUNDAY

We have to reach out and love one another, no matter what. Jesus did. And you can, too. That's just who you are. And when you encounter mean people, pray for them and for the conversion of their hearts. A good way to begin your prayer is to offer them a smile.

Monday

Kindness is the language of the heart that resonates in every soul. Whenever you can, speak heart-to-heart.

Tuesday

It costs nothing to be a nice person, so stop acting like you can't afford a good attitude.

Wednesday

I constantly remind myself to choose my words wisely. To not exercise my freedom of speech until I have exercised my responsibility to think. My words can either heal or hurt, which is why I try to choose them wisely.

Thursday

Fellow Catholics and Christians, always remember that your words, actions, and character are direct reflections of our shared faith. Let us uphold the values and teachings of Jesus Christ so that our lives bring a measure of glory to his name.

Friday

Life's storms vary, but we all are navigating turbulent waters, each in our own way. We can never know what someone else is going through. Kindness and compassion are like anchors in the storms of life; they can be the lifeline that holds someone steady in troubled times.

Saturday

Give without remembering, and receive without forgetting.

CHALLENGE #32

Jesus Christ is the same yesterday and today and forever.

Hebrews 13:8

TRUST IS BOTH A FEELING AND A CHOICE. WHEN WE DON'T feel like we can trust God is the most important time to choose to trust God. But what does it mean to trust God with all your heart? It means to trust deep and wide. Deep—from the surface all the way to the bottom of a concern or situation. Not reserving any part of the effort or outcome. Letting our whole heart's confidence rest primarily and fundamentally in God. Wide—with all things in life, from the menial to the incredibly important. Not reserving any concern we hold in our heart from that trust. After all, God loves us so closely and intimately, he knows the number of hairs on our head. Trusting God with all our heart means choosing to rely on God's love and wisdom, deep and wide.

THIS WEEK'S CHALLENGE:
Expand your trust in God, deep and wide, with a simple prayer: *I want to trust you with this, God. Please help me.*
That's a prayer God never fails to answer.

SUNDAY

I have been accused of sometimes not "acting like a Christian." Well, my friends, God isn't looking for actors; he's looking for authenticity. Others can pass judgment; don't worry about them. Keep your focus on your personal relationship with God, and live out your faith as your genuine self.

Monday

A lot of problems would disappear if we talked *to* one another instead of *about* one another!

Tuesday

When I was younger, I used to admire intelligent people. As I grow older, I admire kind people. What personal traits do you admire most?

Wednesday

God didn't promise days without pain, a lifetime without sorrow, sun without dark nights of the soul. But he did promise strength for the day, comfort for the tears, and light for the way.

Thursday

The gospel is not a product that is tailor-made to fit market demands and consumer preferences. The gospel isn't about conforming to popular opinion. Neither are you.

Friday

Life is a precious gift, but it comes with a simple truth: we can live it only once. So let's make the most of every moment, every opportunity, and every relationship. Live with purpose, love wholeheartedly, and leave a lasting impact that echoes beyond your time on this earth.

Saturday

It's important to talk to God.

CHALLENGE #32
MY 60-SECOND *Reflection*

CHALLENGE #33

Rejoice always, pray without ceasing, give thanks in all

circumstances; for this is the will of God in Christ Jesus for you.

1 Thessalonians 5:16–18

GRATITUDE IS A POWERFUL SPIRITUAL PRACTICE THAT BENEFITS us in spirit, body, and soul. There is an abundance of research showing that the daily practice of intentional gratitude has long-lasting benefits for our health and well-being.

Our attention can easily become hijacked by the concerns of the moment. The work to be done. The worries pressing upon us. Questions. Hopes. Tasks. And screens glaring at us around every turn and in the palm of our hand. See what goodness may come by taking a few moments right now to notice and name those things, people, experiences, and whatever else in your life prompts deep gratitude.

THIS WEEK'S CHALLENGE:
Profess your gratitude deeply and thoroughly
to God and others.

SUNDAY

If you find yourself claiming you don't have time for Jesus, keep in mind that the things you make time for reveal your priorities. Whether it's relationships, work, social media, or leisure activities that are taking up your time, Jesus deserves a prominent place in your daily schedule and in your heart.

Monday

Whenever you're having a bad day, pray for someone else. It will make you feel better, and someone gets a prayer. Win/win.

Tuesday

Remember, peeps: Sometimes God lets us hit rock bottom. It's so that we will discover that he is The Rock at the bottom!

Wednesday

St. Peter observed that people are like grass. Our beauty, he said, is like that of a flower in the field. Grass withers and flowers fade, but the Word of the Lord remains forever (1 Peter 1:24).

Thursday

Let's clarify something important: it's not about your practice of the religion or reciting prayers. It's about the condition of your heart. Jesus longs to meet you right where you are. He longs to embrace you with his unconditional love and grace.

Friday

When you believe in the path you're walking, it shows. You are able to face challenges with passion and enthusiasm. Success follows suit. Winners in life are defined not only by their achievements and end goals but also by their unwavering excitement for the journey itself. Embrace your purpose, but most importantly, embrace the joy along the way.

Saturday

Remember this: Friends come and go. God comes and stays.

MY 60-SECOND *Reflection*

CHALLENGE #34

I give thanks to you, O LORD my God, with my whole heart,

and I will glorify your name forever. Psalm 86:12

"THANK GOD SHE'S OKAY." "THANK GOD NO ONE WAS HURT."
"Thank God I turned the coffee pot off." "Thank God . . ." is
a phrase most of us hear and say quite often. It comes from a
place deep within where we acknowledge the many moments
and situations of our lives for which we owe our thanks to
God's love and protection. "Thank God" can be a wonderful
reminder when we hear it and when we say it.

I had a good friend who said it a little differently. "Thank you,
God," he would say. "Thank you, God, she's okay." "Thank you,
God, no one was hurt." Yes, even, "Thank you, God, I turned
the coffee pot off." At first, his odd phrasing caught me off
guard. But over time, as I heard him—really *heard* him—say
it this way, I realized that there was something powerful in
the slight difference. "Thank you, God" somehow makes it
more real, more personal. More prayerful.

THIS WEEK'S CHALLENGE:
As you encounter your gratitude today, why not give it a
try: Say, "Thank you, God." It's a perfect prayer.

SUNDAY

Love is nurtured by trust, respect, and forgiveness. Love does not happen because we talk about it, but when we live it: it is not a sweet poem to study and memorize but is a life choice to put into practice!

—Pope Francis

Monday

Whenever you feel

unimportant
insecure
lost
alone
forgotten
unworthy
unloved

remember who you belong to—God.

Tuesday

It's important to ignore the ones who talk behind your back. They belong back there, behind you.

Wednesday

Haters are like crickets. Crickets make a lot of noise, and you hear them, but you can't see them. Then right when you walk by them, they go quiet.

Thursday

Yes, we're more aware of our need for God's love, mercy, and help when we have "one of those days." But we can grow even closer to God by searching for how God makes our best days a reality, drinking that in, and saying thank you.

Friday

Whenever you feel swamped or overwhelmed, take a moment to pause. Breathe. Find that inner quiet, and remind yourself that even in the toughest of times, you're never ever walking alone.

Saturday

Joy is what Jesus offers you!

MY 60-SECOND *Reflection*

CHALLENGE #35

I solemnly urge you: proclaim the message; be persistent whether the time is favorable or unfavorable; convince, rebuke, and encourage, with the utmost patience in teaching. 2 Timothy 4:1–2

MANY SPIRITUAL TRADITIONS HAVE PRACTICES TO "SANCTIFY the day." In some countries you can hear calls to prayer at specific times throughout the day as a guide inviting the people to prayer. You might have even heard church bells ringing in odd, longer patterns throughout the day—traditionally six in the morning, noontime, and six in the evening. Known as the "Angelus" bells, they invite the faithful into a moment of prayer and meditation on the Good News announcing the coming of Jesus that the angel (*angelus*) brought to Mary.

There are many resources available for learning and praying this traditional Catholic prayer. But whether you are Catholic or another religious tradition, intentionally giving your whole day to God who loves you does indeed make a difference in your life.

THIS WEEK'S CHALLENGE:
What do you hope will be the result of making your entire day holy in this way? God hears that hope.

SUNDAY

Your journey, marked by hesitant steps and occasional stumbles, is a testament to God's work in your life. Embrace it, share it, inspire and uplift others with your story of resilience and faith, because with God, we may stumble, but we will not fall.

Monday

Sadly, sometimes you see a
person's true colors when you
are no longer beneficial
to their life.

Tuesday

Everyone talks about leaving
the planet a better place for
our kids. Let's also try to leave
better kids for our planet.

Wednesday

Extra shirt? That spare dollar?
Those shoes you never use?
That jacket in the back of your
closet? They belong to someone
else who needs them.

Thursday

Your potential isn't defined
by your past but by how you
choose to show up each and
every new day. Let love, faith,
and dedication, a few of the
many attributes God has
blessed you with, be poured
into every new day.

Friday

Remember, peeps: Anxiety is
like a direct message to God
saying, "I don't think you have
my best interests in mind." But
we can choose to trust God,
knowing he always has our best
interests in mind.

Saturday

Laughter is holy—it's the echo of God's joy in our lives.

CHALLENGE #36

By contrast, the fruit of the Spirit is love, joy, peace, patience,

kindness, generosity, faithfulness, gentleness, and self-control.

There is no law against such things. Galatians 5:22–23

HEROES, THE ONES IN COMIC BOOKS AND ON BIG SCREENS, and the ones who go unnoticed in everyday life, sometimes get discouraged. Take a moment to consider that. Who's your favorite hero? Is there a part of their story when it's all just too much and they want to give up, or turn around, or simply stop?

If you happen to be feeling depleted or at the end of your rope, you're in good company—real and fictional. But good company unfortunately doesn't take away the exhaustion and sense of overwhelm. My prayer is that knowing you're not alone gives you hope. You might not wear a cape, but you do play a key role in God's ministry. And just like the heroes who tap into their source of power when they most need it, you, too, can tap into God's love to fuel you when times get tough.

THIS WEEK'S CHALLENGE:
Consider the times when you've felt worn out
or worn down. Maybe today is one of those times.
Consider this question: What role does God play in
those moments of your life?

I pray for more compassion.

I pray for less anger and more listening.

I pray for less shouting and more forgiveness.

I pray for more understanding and less condemnation.

I pray for this country I love and for peace among all nations.

In Jesus' name. Amen.

Monday

You don't have a right to the cards you believe you should have been dealt. You have an obligation to play the hell out of the ones you're holding.

Tuesday

Spreading love is like making the sign of the cross—it's simple yet profound, and it touches every aspect of our lives.

Wednesday

Faith is like a smartphone battery—it needs daily recharging to keep us connected.

Thursday

We forget to pray when we don't need hope. We fail to pray when we've lost hope. But isn't this when we need prayer the most? You know what will help? A habit of prayer. What if we just prayed every time we stood up, sat down, got a cup of coffee, or—fill in the blank?

Friday

Sometimes life feels like a never-ending climb up a treacherous mountain. The struggle can be so real that we might even forget it was ever any different. But every great adventure story ever told includes peaks and valleys. If we reclaim where we're heading, we'll remember that life—every moment—is a precious gift.

Saturday

Don't worry about tomorrow. God's already there.

....

....

....

....

....

....

....

....

....

....

....

....

....

....

....

....

....

....

CHALLENGE #37

"And the king will answer them, 'Truly I tell you, just as you did

it to one of the least of these who are members of my family,

you did it to me.'" Matthew 25:40

YOU ARE MOST PRECIOUS TO GOD. I WONDER IF YOU ARE truly aware of your worth, to others, to yourself, to God. Sometimes it can be difficult to remember that. Regardless of your personal ministry, your vocation, or how your purpose contributes to God's greater plan, you are worthy of God's love just because you are you.

God doesn't walk with you only so you can care for others or because of what you can "do." God walks with you and keeps you because he loves you for who you *are*. It is your life, your being, that God most desires to strengthen, encourage, and protect. Psalm 121:7 reassures us, "The LORD will keep you from all evil; he will keep your life." The LORD will keep you simply because, to God, you are worth it.

THIS WEEK'S CHALLENGE:
As you go through your days, this week and every week, remember that you are precious to God just for who you are. Keep God's love for you close at heart.

SUNDAY

On this Sunday, let us pray a prayer that we remain mindful of the many gifts God is showering down upon us.

Name them.

And then give thanks for them.

Monday

Remember that you can find happiness in even the darkest of times, if you only remember to turn on the light.

Tuesday

I'm a failure. He's my forgiver.

I'm a sinner. He's my savior.

I'm broken. He's my healer.

I'm his child. He's my God.

Wednesday

The most sacred places on earth are often found in the quiet corners of our daily lives, where love takes the simplest form.

Thursday

Decide to have a great day no matter what comes your way. The secret is: you get to choose! No matter what happens around you today, *you* get to choose what happens *inside you* today! Choose faith. Choose hope. Choose happiness. Choose to pray for me and for others.

Friday

Jesus said everything could be boiled down to two simple notions: love God, and love your neighbor. That's what Jesus did, but even more, that's who Jesus was and is. Sometimes we get focused on wanting to make things different—better—for ourselves or others, but if we find and share true love (for ourselves and others), we're playing our part and imitating Jesus.

Saturday

God isn't asking you to figure it out. He's asking you to trust that he already has.

CHALLENGE #38

Ever since the creation of the world his eternal power and divine

nature, invisible though they are, have been understood and

seen through the things he has made. So they are without excuse.

Romans 1:20

JESUS TAUGHT US TO PRAY "THY KINGDOM COME, THY WILL BE done, on earth as it is in heaven." What a beautiful idea! And what a wonderful way to direct our work and our relationships! God's kingdom and will are about healing, wholeness, love, and community. We know heaven is an eternal experience of that very reality. But so many of our moments here on earth can seem distant from that idea.

What are you doing today to help inch this earth closer to how things are in heaven? And before feeling deflated or defensive, consider the past few hours of your day. Can you celebrate with God those ways you have been a part of healing, wholeness, camaraderie, and love? That's prayer—prayer that can be a funnel from heaven that sustains you for the next hours of working with God.

THIS WEEK'S CHALLENGE:
God's handiwork is all around you. Take time this week
to consider this, and appreciate the beauty of creation.

SUNDAY

Someone asked me, "When did you become a priest?" I responded, "On paper or in my heart?"

Think about that!

Similarly, ask yourself,

When did I become a

Catholic and a Christian?

On paper and in my heart?

Monday

Ponder: I bet purgatory is like trying to get fitted sheets on mattresses with one corner continually popping off.

Tuesday

Treating people right is more important than reciting Bible verses or posting them on social media every day, especially when you don't even practice them.

Wednesday

Our founding fathers may have opted for separation of church and state but not for separation of God and state!

Thursday

Extra Ecclesiam nulla salus is an ancient principle of Catholicism. Before he was elected pope, Cardinal Ratzinger explained this idea wonderfully: "Yes, the church is necessary for salvation. But the church is Jesus, the One Mediator. And his grace can extend as far and wide as Jesus wishes. And oh, my friends, he wishes."

Friday

A compassionate heart is like a church that's open 24/7: always ready to welcome, comfort, and extend God's love. It's an oasis of kindness where every soul can find solace, acceptance, and the warm embrace of community.

Saturday

When things go wrong, don't go wrong with them.

CHALLENGE #39

So if anyone is in Christ, there is a new creation:

everything old has passed away; see, everything has become new!

2 Corinthians 5:17

IN A STORY ATTRIBUTED TO THE LETTERS OF MICHELANGELO, the famed Florentine sculptor Donatello visited a marble quarry in search of the perfect material for his next creation. He rejected a massive block of marble because to his keen eye the flaws, imperfections, and fault lines were obvious. The block of marble went unsold for more than fifty years.

That same block of marble was used by Michelangelo to sculpt the magnificent *David*. It was not that Michelangelo didn't see the marble's imperfections; instead, he knew he could work with them. The story continues that there was a little boy who used to stop by Michelangelo's workshop to watch the artist's progress. One day, there in rough form was *David*. The boy asked, "How did you know there was a man inside that block of marble?" Michelangelo responded, "It was easy. All I had to do was chip away what was not David."

THIS WEEK'S CHALLENGE:
Like Michelangelo, God recognizes our flaws and faults, even as he chips away at all that is not authentically you. Let God's chisel shape you.

SUNDAY

Nobody will remember your salary. Your fancy title. How busy you were. How stressed you were. How many hours you worked. People will remember the time you spent with them. How you made them feel. Whether you kept your promises. If you were there for them. Keep everything in perspective.

Monday

The word to live by today: God's grace is sufficient! Learn it. Apply it. Live by it. That's all. That's enough!

Tuesday

Before you read between the lines, read the actual lines, and learn to get those right. Take this as a reminder to dust off your Bible.

Wednesday

We can throw stones, complain about them, stumble on them, climb over them, or build with them. Start building!

Thursday

Did you really have a bad day? Or did you have ten to twenty minutes when you let your thoughts run down a negative path that you allowed to carry you too far? You're always just a moment away from turning your thoughts back around to the positive. Come on—you got this. Pay attention.

Friday

Did you know that Noah stayed in the ark for over one year? It rained for only forty days, but the flood didn't recede for another eleven months. The takeaway lesson from this story is that recovery takes time. Stay in the boat!

Saturday

For people who unnecessarily hit "reply all" on every email, we pray to the Lord.

MY 60-SECOND *Reflection*

CHALLENGE #40

Depart from evil, and do good; seek peace, and pursue it.

Psalm 34:14

A WISE WOMAN ONCE ENCOURAGED AND CHALLENGED ME BY pointing out that I would contribute energy to every situation or circumstance I encountered in life. "The question is whether you will contribute discord, chaos, hurt, or turmoil, on the one hand, or concord, peace, healing, comfort, and calm, on the other." At first, I was doubtful, but I've found her words to be true.

Being a peacemaker is less about any particular action or comment and more about a way of living life. A manner of being. Even when we don't get it right all the time, we can strive to embrace these ways. Jesus promises that the peacemakers will see God. And that's not just a promise for the future. As I reflect on those situations where I've tried to bring God's love, and tried to be a channel of concord, peace, and healing, I find that there have been encounters with God right in those moments.

THIS WEEK'S CHALLENGE:
What energy will you bring to the situations and circumstances you encounter today? May you bring, and be, a source of God's love and peace.

SUNDAY

The beginning of love is to let those we love be perfectly themselves, and not to twist them to fit our own image. Otherwise, we love only the reflection of ourselves we find in them.

—*Thomas Merton*

Monday

Someone will always be better looking. Someone will always be smarter. Someone will always be younger. But they will never be you. Thank God!

Tuesday

A Scottish proverb: Do not judge by appearances; a rich heart may be under a poor coat.

Wednesday

Your talent is God's gift to you. What you do with it is your gift back to God. Give back to God in abundance.

Thursday

We can be our own worst critic. Some of the best advice I ever heard was a question: "What if you said things to yourself, and treated yourself, the way you would a dear friend?" That's how Jesus wants to treat us, if only we will let him. Another golden piece of wisdom came to me from a fish. Her name is Dory. She advises, "Just keep swimming."

Friday

Does the guest set the invitation list, the dress code, the menu, or the venue? But how much time and energy are we spending doing just that when it comes to the gospel? How different would we be if we focused instead on preparing ourselves, making room for all, and enjoying what the Host has prepared?

Saturday

There is only one rule for being a good talker: Be a good listener.

. . . .

. . . .

. . . .

. . . .

. . . .

. . . .

. . . .

. . . .

. . . .

. . . .

. . . .

. . . .

. . . .

. . . .

. . . .

. . . .

CHALLENGE #41

For who is greater, the one who is at the table or the one who serves?

Is it not the one at the table? But I am among you

as one who serves. Luke 22:27

A TIME MANAGEMENT CONSULTANT TRAVELED THE COUNTRY working with top executives as well as assembly-line workers. He had a gift for sizing up any process and making it more efficient and productive. One day, he told his colleagues of an experience he had at home. For several days, he observed how his wife prepared his breakfast. Each morning it took her exactly twenty minutes. He noticed that she took countless trips between the refrigerator, stove, sink, and table. After four days, the consultant sat his wife down and explained how she could get the same breakfast ready for him with less effort in half the time. He told his colleagues, "Now I get my breakfast in only eight minutes." His colleagues were impressed. "And how many trips does your wife make?" "Zero. I make my own breakfast now."

THIS WEEK'S CHALLENGE:
Observe whether you are offering correction and direction in areas of your life when you could instead be offering gratitude and affirmation.

SUNDAY

We get off track when we see only what we do not have—no way across the Red Sea, only a few loaves and fish. Lucky for us, God works miracles by pointing out to us what we do have. In the miracle stories, a bit of gratitude becomes more than enough. That's the power of gratitude.

Monday

Everyone needs to take this to heart: actions speak louder than words, so believe what you see and forget what you heard.

Tuesday

As a Catholic, when people insult me, I just reply, "And also with you."

Wednesday

To all those in leadership: every one of our hierarchies should be aware that the strong always have something to strive for and the weak have nothing to run from.

Thursday

Question: What's the basic difference between Peter and Judas? Answer: How they responded to having betrayed Jesus. In success and in failure, in virtue and in vice, exhibiting love as best we can and responding in ways that draw us closer to God always makes the difference.

Friday

It's easy to pass judgment, explain, or call a spade a spade. But does that ever really lead to conversion or a deeper relationship? Jesus asked interesting questions: "How many husbands do you have?" He gave radical challenges: "That's right, whoever hasn't sinned should cast the first stone." Jesus led by example: "Follow me, and I will make you fishers of men." That's the difference between judging and inspiring.

Saturday

We are diverse by God's divinity. We are all loved by God's desire!

CHALLENGE #42

Submit yourselves therefore to God. Resist the devil, and he will flee from you. Draw near to God, and he will draw near to you.

James 4:7–8

ACCORDING TO THE CUSTOM AND PRACTICE OF THE JEWISH people at the time, Joseph and Mary took Jesus to the temple a little over a month after he was born. Mary knew that Jesus was God himself—God who came to be with us. Be one of us. So why follow this ritual? Obedience, for one. Jesus, Mary, and Joseph lived lives of obedience to God. Community is another reason. It is good and important and even holy to exercise and reinforce our belonging to one another with rituals and traditions. There is a third important reason the family went to present Jesus at the temple. They wanted to offer to God the journey before them. What they brought to the temple, they offered up to God. Like wrapping a precious gift and giving it to a loved one, only deeper.

You, too, are precious to God. You, too, have gifts, talents, and a miraculous life.

> **THIS WEEK'S CHALLENGE:**
> What's it like to offer all of "that"—which is to say, all of you—to God?

SUNDAY

Imagine how fruitful our Church would be if we defended Jesus as much as we defended political candidates. Boom! There it is! Let your thoughts and conversations dwell on the Good News of our Lord and not on the news of the world.

Monday

Remember something, peeps: In the age of social media, be as quick to kneel as you are to text, tweet, and post.

Tuesday

Strong? No, my friend, I am far from it. What you are seeing is simply a weak person with a very strong God.

Wednesday

Yes, Jesus wept. We often forget that he also smiled and laughed and was filled with joy. Serve the Lord with laughter and a joyful heart.

Thursday

When you look at people who seem to be "the others"—the incarcerated, the homeless, the poor, or the very wealthy— what do you feel? Chances are these feelings reflect your insecurities about whether God can, or does, or will, love you. But, you see, in God's eyes, *everyone* is sacred and worthy of love.

Friday

The key is to remember that hope isn't a feeling but a choice. To hope when you're not feeling hopeful simply means to choose faith in God, and trust that his love and goodness ensures that he is working for our good. Yes, we can lose sight of goodness and hope. But we can also always go looking for them again.

Saturday

Try sending a prayer to God more quickly than sending a text message to friends!

MY 60-SECOND *Reflection*

. . . .

. . . .

. . . .

. . . .

. . . .

. . . .

. . . .

. . . .

. . . .

. . . .

. . . .

. . . .

. . . .

. . . .

. . . .

. . . .

. . . .

. . . .

. . . .

CHALLENGE #43

"But the Advocate, the Holy Spirit, whom the Father will send in my name, will teach you everything, and remind you of all that I have said to you." John 14:26

IT'S EASY TO LEAD A SEGMENTED LIFE. IN FACT, SO MANY OF THE norms and requirements of our work life require us to dive into our work roles and manage interpersonal interactions differently depending on the context. At work, with friends, and at home, these interactions serve a necessary and important purpose.

But they also make it easier to create segments of life where relying on God, trusting God, and acknowledging God for who God is and the role God plays get forgotten. Faith in God isn't something that's just for worship service or private moments of prayer. Trusting in God is as necessary in the office as it is at home with family. Yes, trust may need to be lived and expressed differently depending on the context. But acknowledging God is equally important no matter the situation, the group, or the person.

> **THIS WEEK'S CHALLENGE:**
> As you walk with God this week, invite him to raise your awareness of how to acknowledge him in the different streams of your life. What a great way to grow with God!

SUNDAY

You've probably heard the saying "God gives us only what we can handle." Apparently, then, God thinks I'm a badass! As you reflect this week, consider the many strengths God has blessed you with so that you can overcome any obstacle on your journey toward him.

Monday

We are not supposed to change any part of the gospel. The gospel is supposed to change every part of us.

Tuesday

If it happens once, it's a mistake. If it happens twice, it's a choice. Read that again. Got it? Now apply it.

Wednesday

I do not want a Catholic Church that will move with the world. I want a Catholic Church that will move the world.

Thursday

The Christian life is lived squarely at the threshold of past and future, not on either side of it. Where are you today? Where is God today? Finding and embracing where you are in relation to God in this moment is key.

Friday

From Genesis to Revelation, the whole story is God's relationship with his people. Even the adventures of just one person—Jonah, Ruth, Noah, Moses, Paul, Mary Magdalene—are somehow related to God seeking relationship with "us." Yes, a personal relationship with Jesus is important and meaningful, but there is no relationship with Jesus that is purely "me"; in one way or another, it is always also "we."

Saturday

Remember something, peeps: If your Bible is in good shape, you aren't! Think about it!

MY 60-SECOND *Reflection*

CHALLENGE #44

I will instruct you and teach you the way you should go;

I will counsel you with my eye upon you. Psalm 32:8

IF WE TRUST GOD DEEP AND WIDE, MAKING ROOM FOR GOD'S love and wisdom to work along with our understanding, then God will direct our paths. It can seem like this is a trade-off, a payment that God gives us in exchange for trusting him. The truth is, God isn't a merchant like that. God doesn't so much reward us for trusting him as he loves us enough to step back when we crowd him out. This is less about transaction and more about God's love and wisdom persistently at work in and around us as much as we will allow.

I suppose there are times it can seem like we don't want God guiding and directing us. We want to be driving the car. Truthfully, God loves us enough to give us that freedom. But choosing to trust God illuminates the road ahead so that our relationships, our purpose, and the journey of life go much more smoothly, and gets us safely back home with him.

THIS WEEK'S CHALLENGE:
What aspects of your life are you gripping too tightly, as we do when we are white-knuckling the steering wheel? How might you let God's light improve your journey?

SUNDAY

One night the Lord spoke to Paul in a vision, telling him that he should not be afraid, and that he should not remain silent, but keep on speaking out. (Acts 18:9)

What is God saying to you today?

What is God beckoning you to do?

How will you respond to God's invitation?

Monday

Press on. Obstacles are seldom the same size tomorrow as they are today. This is especially true when we pray.

Tuesday

Here are some words of support: Trust in the Lord with all your heart. Lean not on your own understanding. Leave your fear behind. The Lord is with you.

Wednesday

God loves you as much on your worst day as he does on your best day.

Thursday

Hungry, angry, lonely, tired, stressed—these all-too-human sensations tend to make us turn inward. They leave us looking downward and feeling stifled. But when we look up and around, we find God. And there's no better way to refresh and recharge than by serving God through serving someone else.

Friday

It's always worth remembering that God's Word, most perfectly expressed, is a person: Jesus Christ. A person who calls us family even when we act more like enemy or stranger. A person who gives all, without hesitation, as an expression of love for us. How different would today be if we put Jesus at the center of our day?

Saturday

No one can drive us crazy unless we give them the key!

....

....

....

....

....

....

....

....

....

....

....

....

....

....

....

....

CHALLENGE #45

*Trust in the L*ORD *with all your heart,*

and do not rely on your own insight. Proverbs 3:5

IN THE CLAMOR OF MODERN LIFE, WE OFTEN FIND OURSELVES in need of guidance, purpose, and peace. Yet, we tend to overlook the obvious, profound truth that communicating with Jesus requires nothing more than an open heart. The quietude of prayer and serenity of contemplation create a sacred space where dialogue with Jesus takes root. This interaction involves accepting an invitation to trust, embracing divine love and wisdom, and allowing Jesus to illuminate our path.

When we steer the wheel of life ourselves, Jesus grants us the freedom to choose our course. However, if we trust in him, our journey is transformed. With every step taken in faith, we draw closer to Jesus. Through this intimate communion, our hearts resonate with his wisdom, guidance, and boundless love, and we navigate life with grace.

THIS WEEK'S CHALLENGE:
Every day this week, take a moment to quiet your mind by focusing on your breath. Ask God to come into your heart and direct your actions. Repeat this simple prayer: *Jesus, lead me by the heart.*

SUNDAY

A conversation with God doesn't require a grand cathedral. An open heart is the only sanctuary you need. It's in the soft whispers of prayer, the quiet moments of contemplation, and even in the daily hustle and bustle of life that we can feel his divine presence.

Monday

For every minute you are angry, you lose sixty seconds of happiness.

Tuesday

Not because of who I am, but because of what God's done.

Not because of what I've done, but because of who God is.

Wednesday

While I was doing some research, I came across this little piece of wisdom from writer and businessperson Paul Boese: "Forgiveness doesn't change the past, but it does enlarge our future."

Thursday

Faith isn't a set of Sunday china to be used for special occasions. It should be our daily dishware—sturdy, reliable, always ready to serve up heaping portions of love and generosity to those around us.

Friday

Being a disciple isn't about clocking in holy hours. It's about making each hour holy by filling it with acts of kindness, choosing compassion, and leaning into God's grace.

Saturday

Forgiveness is like old, fine wine—it may take time, but it's worth the wait.

CHALLENGE #46

"For if you forgive others their trespasses, your heavenly Father will also forgive you; but if you do not forgive others, neither will your Father forgive your trespasses." Matthew 6:14–15

"FORGIVE US OUR TRESPASSES AS WE FORGIVE THOSE WHO trespass against us." We recite these words countless times in our lives, but they are easier said than done. Especially when we feel we have been treated unjustly or harmed deliberately, forgiveness is difficult. But God, who desires peace among his people, wants us to keep trying. As we seek his mercy and compassion for our wrongdoings, we must extend those same graces to those who have wronged us.

Learning to love unconditionally with the love, acceptance, and grace of Jesus coincides with learning how to forgive. If we really want to love, truly, we must learn how to forgive.

THIS WEEK'S CHALLENGE:
Who in your life has wronged you? Whether the trespass against you was as slight as being cut off in traffic or as significant as a profound emotional wound from someone close to you, forgive them. For them, yes, but mostly for yourself. Whether you speak directly to them or grant forgiveness in the quiet of your own heart, forgive them.

SUNDAY

Jesus' stories provide examples of who we want to be as well as who we don't want to be—like the son who returns to the father seeking forgiveness, and the other son who was jealous because the return of his brother was celebrated. As we pray for difficult people, let those people guide who we choose to be for Christ.

M o n d a y

Remember, peeps: To be a Christian means to forgive the inexcusable, because God has forgiven the inexcusable in you. Bam!

T u e s d a y

Learn how to forgive quickly, frequently, and thoroughly. Forgiveness takes one. Reconciliation takes two.

W e d n e s d a y

I am a Christian who is Catholic. That does not mean I am perfect—just forgiven.

T h u r s d a y

One of our biggest obstacles to experiencing God's forgiveness is filtering it through our own ways of forgiving. And the primary challenge to forgiving quickly and frequently is that we often don't forgive completely. Does Jesus truly and completely forgive us? Yes—it's wiped clean. Practice this kind of forgiveness as if you were learning to play an instrument, and see how deeply you come to realize just how forgiven you are.

F r i d a y

He laid down on the cross because they couldn't have put him there unless he let them. With arms stretched wide, hands held open, the spike poised over the center of his palm. And as they drove the nail into his hand, Jesus thought, *Father, avenge me!* No, actually, he didn't. He said, "Father, forgive them." Redemption comes through forgiveness.

S a t u r d a y

Forgive, even when it's hard!

CHALLENGE #47

"And forgive us our debts, as we also have forgiven our debtors."

Matthew 6:12

THERE IS NO SUCH THING AS A "PRIVATE" SIN. IN ONE WAY OR another, our mistakes hurt someone else. A child's innocent observation about the biblical concept of trespassing highlights this truth: "Why were people running around on someone else's farm all the time?" The child had something right. When we sin, break trust, take what isn't ours, and hurt or harm others, we are "running around on someone else's farm."

But God's love is all about mercy and forgiveness. We know and embrace that. The tough part is remembering that God asks us—expects us—to be as forgiving with others as he is with us. What a wonderful moment in this prayer to let God open our eyes to how, and with whom, we can be more like our forgiving God.

> **THIS WEEK'S CHALLENGE:**
> How and with whom
> can you be more forgiving?

SUNDAY

It's often said that the mission of the Church is to save souls, but certainly a richer way to express that is to say that the mission of the Church is to create circumstances in which Jesus can save souls. In those circumstances, the strongest, Jesus, carries the weakest, us, over and through the dangers.

Monday

May I never forget, on my best day, that I need God as desperately as I did on my worst day.

Tuesday

Oh, yes, when people look down on you because you aren't who they want you to be, that's when you know you are doing something right.

Wednesday

As we struggle through good days and bad, we remember that Jesus never said it would be easy. He said it would be worth it!

Thursday

Life itself is motion. In fact, perfect relationship and perpetual exchange of love—movement—are defining characteristics of God. And we are, after all, truly *imago Dei*, created in the image of God. So there is going to be movement—things are always changing. Growth is when we allow that change to propel and sanctify us as we grow more and more into God's image.

Friday

I don't just believe in Jesus:

I worship him.
I trust him.
I love him.
I follow him.
I preach him.
I share him.
I serve him.
I'm his disciple.

Saturday

Speak the truth, even if your voice shakes.

CHALLENGE #48

*Oh give thanks to the L*ORD*, for he is good; for his steadfast love*

*endures forever. Let the redeemed of the L*ORD *say so, those he*

redeemed from trouble and gathered in from the lands, from

the east and from the west, from the north and from the south.

Psalm 107:1–3

I'M OFTEN STRUCK BY THE DEPTH OF MEANING THAT CAN come from careful attention to language. One example is our word in English for the holiday we celebrate in November, Thanksgiving. In common usage, the word mostly describes the day we feast with family and friends. In the best of times, it is a celebration of all we have to be grateful for.

In Spanish, "Thanksgiving" is *acción de gracias*, literally "action of thanks." This perspective adds depth to something we often take for granted. As you reflect on gratitude, consider how you can incorporate an "action of thanks" with each of your thoughts of appreciation.

THIS WEEK'S CHALLENGE:
Reflect on the difference between *thanks* and *giving thanks*. Then propel your thanksgiving into action. To your family. To your loved ones. To random people you encounter in your day. Perform actions of thanks!

SUNDAY

True joy comes from a profound harmony between persons, something which we all feel in our hearts and which makes us experience the beauty of togetherness, of mutual support along life's journey.

—*Pope Francis*

Monday

The divine is in the details; in every "Thank you" said, in every helping hand, in every moment of patience amid the hustle and bustle of our daily lives. Tune in to the details.

Tuesday

Celebrate each step, every progress, no matter the size. In God's eyes, every effort toward love and kindness is a triumph.

Wednesday

Your current chapter isn't the end of your story. With God as your guide, the best is yet to come.

Thursday

This year I want to be more like Jesus. I want to hang out with sinners. Upset religious people. Tell stories that make people think. Choose unpopular friends. Be kind, loving, and merciful. Take naps on boats.

Friday

Some people could be given an entire field of roses and only see the thorns in it. Others could be given a field of weeds and only see the wildflowers in it. Perception is a key component of gratitude, and gratitude is a key component of joy.

Saturday

God loves you. God also loves that person you don't like.

CHALLENGE #49

As God's chosen ones, holy and beloved, clothe yourselves with

compassion, kindness, humility, meekness, and patience.

Colossians 3:12

WE ALL FACE PRESSURE AT CERTAIN POINTS IN OUR LIVES. Nurses, surgeons, and first responders experience pressure that can literally have life-altering consequences. For others, a deadline at work or crushing financial burden might be a source of stress. The important thing to consider is whether your pressures rob you of kindness, patience, and your ability to be loving in your relationships.

Mother Teresa advised, "I prefer you to make mistakes in kindness than work miracles in unkindness." No, that's not me wishing you or any of us a moment of carelessness as we go about our work and when we next face mounting pressures. It's just a perceptive reminder from this selfless woman who accomplished so much good. A reminder that giving and receiving kindness can be as powerful as a miracle.

THIS WEEK'S CHALLENGE:
When you face pressures, however big or small,
observe how they affect your loving-kindness
toward others.

SUNDAY

In moments of happiness, let kindness overflow from your heart. When anger flares up, let kindness be your response. Whether excitement fills your spirit or frustration tests your patience, choose kindness as your constant companion. In a world where you can be anything, be kind.

Monday

Be a good person. Love who you can, help where you can, and give what you can.

Tuesday

Every act of kindness and every word of comfort are seeds of God's love. Keep sowing, and watch his blessings bloom all around you.

Wednesday

Blessed are the flexible, for they shall not be bent out of shape.

Thursday

Thank you, God, for a lifetime of laughter. For a lifetime of family and friendships. For a lifetime of love. For a lifetime of overcoming struggles. For a lifetime of joy. For a lifetime you gave me as a precious gift. I am grateful for each moment. Thank you, God. Amen.

Friday

It's no coincidence that the Scriptures encourage us to love our neighbor (and ourselves), and to keep our eyes and hearts leaning forward without looking back. How many times did Jesus say, "Be not afraid"? That's because hate, regret, and fear pull us down and back, while God's spirit always pulls us up and forward.

Saturday

Remember that a saint is a sinner who keeps trying.

MY 60-SECOND *Reflection*

. . . .

. . . .

. . . .

. . . .

. . . .

. . . .

. . . .

. . . .

. . . .

. . . .

. . . .

. . . .

. . . .

. . . .

CHALLENGE #50

He asked that he might die: "It is enough; now, O LORD, take away my life, for I am no better than my ancestors." Then he lay down under the broom tree and fell asleep. Suddenly an angel touched him and said to him, "Get up and eat." 1 Kings 19:4–5

THE MARK OF A TRUE HERO IS, OF COURSE, GOING THE DISTANCE. But we can't overlook that heroes also take opportunities to rest. The prophet Elijah felt so burdened that he was ready to give up. What did he do? He sat down under a broom tree and fell asleep. And that led to an encounter that helped him make it the rest of the way.

You probably don't have a broom tree nearby for you to nap under in your day-to-day life. And you might be so busy that naps are hard to come by. But the point here is that it is heroic to seek and find moments of rest. Step away for a minute just to close your eyes and breathe deeply. Give yourself a moment to think of loved ones, good times, anything that can lift your spirit. These moments of rest are important spiritual practices for a hero like you.

THIS WEEK'S CHALLENGE:
This week, take some quiet moments to rest, recharge, and, if you can't snag a nap, at least have a snack!

SUNDAY

Rest is so necessary for the health of our minds and bodies, and often so difficult to achieve due to the many demands placed on us. But rest is also essential for our spiritual health, so that we can hear God's voice and understand what he asks of us.

—*Pope Francis*

Monday

Being challenged in life is inevitable. Being defeated is optional. In God we trust.

Tuesday

Do not get caught up in the how, when, and why of God; get caught up in trusting him.

Wednesday

When Elijah professed, "God, I'm so mad I want to die!" God said, "Here is some food. Why don't you have a nap?" So Elijah slept, ate, and decided things weren't so bad after all. Never underestimate the spiritual power of a snack and a nap.

Thursday

Rules for life:

Express gratitude.
Keep your promises.
Say "I love you."
Speak the truth.
Use kind words.
Consider others.
Do your best.
Pray.

Friday

Jacob slept over stones. Elijah slept under a broom tree. Daniel slept in a lions' den. Jonah slept in a ship. Peter slept in a prison. Eutychus slept on a windowsill. Jesus slept during a storm. So, no matter your situation, you can probably take a nap today. I know I will!

Saturday

Worry will wear you out. The word of God will work it out.

MY 60-SECOND *Reflection*

CHALLENGE #51

Devote yourselves to prayer, keeping alert in it with thanksgiving.

Colossians 4:2

How to Pray the Examen:

1. Place yourself in God's presence. Give thanks for God's love for you.
2. Pray for the grace to understand how God is acting in your life.
3. Review your day. Recall specific moments.
4. Ask yourself: Did I draw closer to God or move farther away?
5. Look toward tomorrow, and make a plan to better collaborate with God. Conclude with the Our Father.

Praying St. Ignatius's Examen is like conducting a daily checkup on your relationship with God.

THIS WEEK'S CHALLENGE:
Pray the Examen throughout this week.
Reflect on the moments you notice, as well as
the moments God notices.

SUNDAY

In Dante's *The Divine Comedy*, the center of hell is frozen, stuck, and turned inward. Negativity is like that, and it pulls everyone down. The antidote is looking up and moving forward. We don't have to push others down to keep our eyes on God and our feet moving forward.

Monday

Remember that no random act of kindness is too small. One simple act can change the life of another in an instant.

Tuesday

The true test of Christianity is not just loving Jesus. The true test is loving Judas.

Wednesday

I fall. I make mistakes. I rise. I live. I learn. I've been hurt. I'm still alive. I'm human. I'm not perfect, but I'm thankful to God for it all. Amen.

Thursday

Words to ponder: Instead of raising our voices in anger, let us elevate our words with kindness, compassion, and understanding. After all, it is rain that helps to make the flowers grow, not thunder.

Friday

Jesus did it over and over. He went where the sinner was, without judgment, and invited a relationship by starting a conversation. So different from expecting the lost to come to us and listen to us preach! Could it be that, without ignoring or condoning the sin, the person Jesus saw was much less a sinner, much more a brother, sister, or friend?

Saturday

Wake up, people! You are breathing, so you are blessed!

CHALLENGE #52

He said to them, "Why were you searching for me? Did you not

know that I must be in my Father's house?" Luke 2:49

FLASH-FORWARD TWELVE YEARS AFTER THE INCARNATION TO when the Holy Family goes to Jerusalem to celebrate Passover. On their way home, Joseph and Mary suddenly realize they can't find Jesus. They've lost him, and not just a little bit. They were a whole day away before they even noticed, and it was three days before they were reunited. (Parents, God gets it. Parenting is hard work!) They found Jesus at the temple. When they asked him what he'd been doing, Jesus replied, "Why did you seek me? Did you not know that I must be about my Father's business?"

Sometimes going about God's business looks to others as if we're lost, or we've been distracted. What's great is when we discover that we've been about God's business and didn't even know it. All who wander are indeed not lost. How have you been about God's business today?

THIS WEEK'S CHALLENGE:
What does it look like when you are going about God's business? Probably a lot like minding your own business while being aligned with God's given purpose. This week, stay diligent, tending to your Father's business.

SUNDAY

Life offers endless possibilities for how you can choose to spend it. The decisions are yours, but remember, time is a currency that cannot be replenished. Make each moment count. Live with intention. Invest your days in pursuits that bring joy and fulfillment. And use your God-given talents to be a blessing to all you encounter.

Monday

Words of mercy: We must throw away our presuppositions about what "God" means and allow Jesus to show us who God is.

Tuesday

If you claim to be someone's ally but aren't getting hit by the stones being thrown at them, then you aren't standing close enough.

Wednesday

A person's most useful asset is not a head full of knowledge but a heart full of love, an ear ready to listen, and a hand willing to help.

Thursday

If you've got time for social media, a boyfriend or girlfriend, watching television, hanging out, or playing video games, then you've certainly got time for Jesus!

Friday

Jesus didn't ignore her sin when the crowd wanted to stone her. He didn't tell her the sin was okay, but he did tell her—and show her—that she was okay. In fact, Jesus didn't even condemn the crowd for their self-righteous judgmentalism. Jesus spoke truth with love—to the woman caught in adultery, to everyone he met, and to you and me. Let's imitate that!

Saturday

The only one qualified to throw a stone . . . didn't.

ABOUT THE AUTHOR

Father Jim Sichko is a traveling Missionary of Mercy for Pope Francis, a priest of the Diocese of Lexington, Kentucky, and the author of multiple books. He travels throughout the United States leading missions, retreats, and days of reflection. Known for his storytelling and selfies, Father Jim weaves together everyday life experiences with the fundamental messages of the Gospel.

Notes

. . . .

. . . .

. . . .

. . . .

. . . .

. . . .

. . . .

. . . .

. . . .

. . . .

. . . .

. . . .

. . . .

. . . .

. . . .

. . . .

Notes

Notes

Notes

Notes